AF382861

Druck und Distribution im Auftrag der Autorin:

tredition GmbH, Heinz-Beusen-Stieg 5, 22926 Ahrensburg, Deutschland

Das Werk, einschließlich seiner Teile, ist urheberrechtlich geschützt. Für die Inhalte ist

die Autorin verantwortlich. Jede Verwertung ist ohne ihre Zustimmung unzulässig. Die

Publikation und Verbreitung erfolgen im Auftrag der Autorin, zu erreichen unter: L. H.

Kuhrau, Straße des Friedens 50, 98724 Lauscha, Germany.

One last

Mistake

L.H. Kuhrau

Preface

Thank you for choosing to read the last book in the "One last..." series. You might have gotten an image of former themes like cancer, addictions, and BDSM, but you will also find those and other existing themes in this book. Prepare yourself for the last mistakes they make, which will lead them to the final solutions and answers they have to find in order to continue with their lives.

While reading the book, please keep in mind that the themes are not written by a specialist, and even if everything is clearly researched, mistakes can occur in the middle.

Please be aware that the following book contains violence, sexual abuse, illnesses like cancer, sexual content, and other contents that might be sensitive to some readers. For further information, please check out the book subscription.

Enjoy the reading!

One last **B**eat

One last **D**eath

One last **S**uffer-ring

One last **M**istake

"We all have the tiny bubble of justice in us,

but its touches make a disaster.

Still, they all touch it."

Part 1

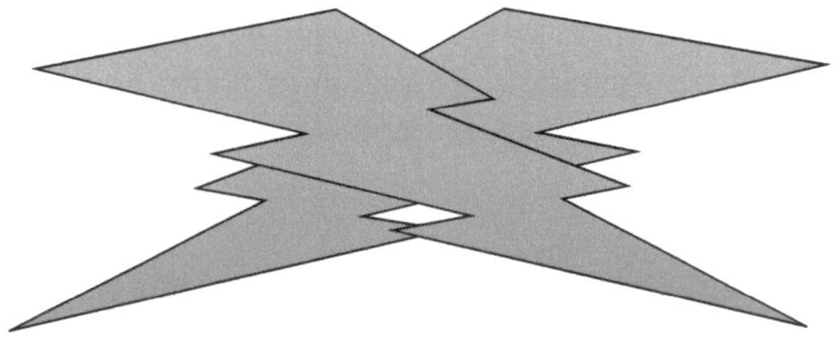

Chapter 1

"Let me drive us," Deen offered, and without another word, Nathaniel sat himself back in the car with me. I saw that his hands were already there shacking. Since he had the chance, he took off as much time as possible to prepare himself for the court, which we were driving to now.

We all knew that it wasn't just a court for him. No. It was what has defined his life: his carrier, his only edge of not being able to have sexual contact with anybody, and of course other traumas that he has. There may be a reason why I have never seen him asleep before. Even if we'd been sleeping beside each other a lot—not only now with Deen in the garage, but already on our holidays each day and sometimes before that too. Almost inhumanly, even if the fact that it was since he is scared for the nightmares is more human than everything else.

Carefully, I took his hand into mine, always unsure if what I did was too much for him. Yes, it's simple handholding, but in a sorrowful situation, he might want to be alone.

Almost too hard, he took it into his arms and squeezed them. He took a short look at me, and I tried to smile comfortingly. It really hurts, almost. However, that wasn't even an idea of how much everything did harm him. I wanted to comfort him by saying some kind words that would calm him, but I didn't have any idea what they might be.

"I love you," I whispered while I leaned towards his shoulder, which comforted me more, and he seemed to relax a little more too. Without a direct answer, just a kiss on my head, we continued to stay in this position.

The drive took almost an unbearable, painful, and silent hour. I had seen that Deen too, even if he hadn't had time the past few weeks to be around us at all, had a tensed face while he knew as much as we all did how important this case would be.

His clinic had started a few weeks ago, and until now, everything has turned out well. It did, as Nathaniel expected, take up most of his time. Therefore, I hadn't seen him more than just in the night since then. It would just be now at the start like that, they had explained, and that it always was alike by starting a new business, and I hope that this is true. To miss him as a workaholic wasn't really anything I wanted. It already seemed to me that I would miss Nathaniel to this judge the past few weeks. Again, I had often been alone. Of course, I didn't blame him. The fact that it would be over soon suited me well too. On the other side, the court had two ways to end: well, and with him working full-time in his own clinic again. Or badly, which wasn't anything I wanted to think about, scared that it would make him lose the stability he had. Throughout his entire life, this has been what he fought for. If we miss and lose such, we change as people, and I am scared that I don't like the way he would change.

The house was larger than I had expected. The press was already everywhere, like the public, which wanted to hear the way the judge turned out to be. It was an important theme for everybody; medicine had gotten so important in our society that almost everybody was dependent on it, which meant that lower costs were something many people supported. Additionally, the curiosity of what else we had to say against them filled many minds. That it wasn't "only" about the high pricing had gotten official and written in many papers.

We went out of the car, and as soon as the public saw us, I didn't see Nathaniel anymore. A mask covered him, excluding all the feelings he had while we were there in privacy.

"We can't enter until now," Deen jogged back to us while we waited on the closed doors. As always, Nathaniel wanted to be as early as possible. An hour earlier was, well, too early.

Deen had changed too; not only had he shortened his hair, but he also seemed more successful and satisfied with himself. He wouldn't laugh out of discomfort or talk just to fill the silence anymore. Therefore, we stood there and waited in silence for it to start.

After about half an hour, some well-dressed men arrived and passed us. Even if I didn't know who was there, I could see a glimmer of guilt in their eyes as they gave us a simple nod before entering the large building.

Why would they feel like they had to be guilty for anything before everything had started? Did they know something that made them imagine the case's end? Wouldn't everything I had gotten to see in the worst weeks of my life be enough to get the pharmacists stopped and punished?

Chapter 2

"Mr. Favouner," I said, reaching for his hand while he nodded firmly. "I am glad you could make it in such a short time." I smiled to lighten his mood so that I was able to read him and figure out if he lied or changed the truth in some way. Stone-hard façade—no chance.

"Without my former clinic, it was easy to make it in a day's time to you, president," he said. He didn't even use my real name, just the rang I had worked for. It was okay, but it showed me that he had already tried to make himself more comfortable with trying to intimate me. It was worth a try, but nobody had succeeded with that. Ever.

We almost challenged ourselves by holding eye contact for as long as possible. He wasn't a softy at all. How could he be? At such a young age, I had been studying, not already a case against the pharmaceutical industry, because he was sure about the fact that they had bombed it down. Possible, but not findable.

"Tell me what exactly has happened and why you weren't at the clinic at the time of the incident," I started, not breaking eye contact or losing a hint of his "emotional changes".

"Already before the event, we had many confrontations. The fact that whose people had the chance to pay the prize of the clinic and were smart enough to see the statistics of it and chose me infront of his industry wasn't likeable for him at all" I frowned while he calmly started to explain the facts. Money. Everything was always either about money or power in these social classes. This was about a huge loss of income for the fav. pharmaceuticals, which they got from the cancer patients.

"I stopped to count somewhere at ten spy's which they sent out. Later, I got to know that some of my patients did work for them too. Desperately, they tried to figure out the medicamentation and ways of curing. Well, they couldn't find anything critical or any cooperation with other pharmaceutical industries, which made them even more furious. To get further information about them, I played the same game. Two of my closest connections stayed there for several weeks. Allowed." He pointed out, but it was still espionage, which they wouldn't get punished for as long as they didn't do anything illicit there.

"The facts that they found out there did even shock me, and trust me, I am not a man who easily gets surprised." I nodded, as I already had figured that out of his person: a realist, which didn't mean that he was a pessimist, but more a rational, calm mind that knew exactly the intensity of the chance he had to win this case.

"I am going to drive to your opponent right after this visit. Is there anything I could prepare him for so that we have equal justice?" I knew that he would answer. Many people didn't want the other one to know anything about the hard things they had figured out, and they almost shocked them with their own acts in curt. However, it wasn't really beneficial for them, as the judge wants to have an equal court and therefore is very against hidden sources and events, which one of the sides knows about.

"I take it as a self-understanding that I also am going to get informed if they do have anything that they would want to use against us in court," he said without any change of expression, not scared, angry, sad, or vulnerable. Just calm, realistic, and decided. I nodded slowly, even if I doubted that they would make it to a fighter case, in which both sides tried to show that they were "better" by using criminalistic acts on each side against each other.

"Name him personally; child abuse, women's suicide, and untested medicaments. I believe that he is well aware of what is meant and doesn't need an explanation about what exactly he has done." I nodded, remaining calmly at the hard facts. There wasn't anything that would shock me, either. Corrupt, illegal, and blackmailing others just to have better chances. The world has always been about power, money, and status and will always remain that way.

The fact that their houses hadn't been longer away from each other than an hour's drive hit me as soon as I came to my second visit. It wouldn't even have been hard for them to transport a bomb to the clinic since they also had further "stations" on the way with testing laboratories. I liked the fact that they accused the PVT clinic of not mentioning the way they healed, and then they themselves surely said what they might do but never would say the truth about it. On the other side, who cared about the truth? As long as people got to know what they wanted to hear, it wasn't about whether it was true or not, but just the calming massage that they "desperately" tried to figure out ways of medicamentation.

Already, the house showed power, wealth, and the status of an pharma industry income. From every sector, the highest said enough about the legality and powerlessness that others had against it. Including the state himself.

Two ladies made their way out of the house as soon as I arrived. My eagle eye catches the fact that there was a hand that pushed them out, not their own stupidity of struggling to go, as one of them fell on her knees and the other one struggled to find her balance again. I wasn't supposed to already see that, but my eyes did catch every fact in a 360-degree view 100% of the time. Stressful, energy-consuming, but unbelievable good in my position. The only fact I liked about home visits was that even if everything was hidden under a silk-white tablecloth, I would still recognise the blood underneath.

"Just go to him, and then he starts to talk to us about, I don't know, if he says anything, just say what your father has told you. Remain calm and relaxed; he's going to help us". Hopefully, they didn't recognise me behind my large black SUV, which made it even easier for me to overhear some facts. Unhelpful facts, then I already saw that even if they hadn't seen me, the surroundings were camera-supervised. You couldn't see anybody throughout the windows, but I could basically feel the eyes on me.

"Good afternoon" I greeted them like they had whished and figured out the most natural way of engaging them into a small chatty conversation—to get to know what her father had wanted them to tell me. Everything could be helpful. Everything had a hint and a purpose for me to know. Even if it wasn't supposed to be one, I would figure it out and read the simple greeting as a showing of fear, helplessness, or even as a cry for help. It was just about watching, hearing, and reading them. Nobody would believe me about this ability as long as they haven't figured it out themselves. Unrecognisable, aged, and seemingly uninterested while being interested. Centuries of learning and working had taught me that it wasn't helpful to intimidate anybody to get further information. They had to relax and think that you're on their side before they would lose their court because of you.

"Isn't it a little cold in November for a bathing trip?" I recognised that they didn't wear anything more than a bikini under the large coat they had taken on themselves.

"Good afternoon. We're on the way to the new swimming pool that opened yesterday," the older one, seemingly the age of a mother to the younger woman, explained. Both had gotten many operations to look like they did; one of them was Botox, the other was plastic surgery, and I don't know how much silicon for the proportions.

"I see, that is exactly the right thing to do on such a cold, almost harmful, freezing day." I had a relaxed smile on myself for comforting them and trying to get them to talk more than the view sentences that they were supposed to say.

A smile and nod, while they both tensed as hell. Not because of me, but I could tell that there was something that knew everything they wanted to say. Cameras could mean that they also listened to what they said. Every day, everywhere, and every time.

"Good day, sir. Mr. Favouner is going to be here in a second," an employed woman said to me kindly, but I already heard other voices as I stood in the entrance area of the building.

"Don't judge him. He's here to judge us. There is a reason that such people are promoted in the state." I heard a whisper while the woman continued to talk to me about what a pleasure it is to meet me in reality and how much she'd heard about me before. Bullshit. Nobody would appreciate me that much; she was just covering or trying to cover the voices that were interesting.

"Wait a second here; I will just inform him about your presence." She smiled kindly, and I nodded charmingly, which made her hurry even faster. She was afraid of male attention, not in want of any, like she had been trying to convince me to believe.

"Mr. Sterling, what a pleasure!" the 6.5-foot-tall accused pharmacist, Doc. Nathaniel Favouner, greeted me with his slicked-back black hair and a little pudgy body by the age of 67. I smiled and tried to seem natural glad to see him too, not as overdriving as he had, since it made it even more obvious to me that he wasn't that interested in having me here at his place. Like he had said earlier to his son, Henry Favouner, who appeared right behind him, the state did have reasons to give me such a position. Imagine that it wasn't even about my earlier status or power in our society; it was just about abilities, something that this man never needed nor had.

"Can I introduce you to my ancestor, Henry Favouner?" He turned a little so that I could face his son easily. We both stepped forward to make a handshake. His hands were ice-cold, while his face also seemed tensed. Not even good at hiding or faking emotions, that wasn't anything good to not be able to do in their industry; everything was about that, nothing else. Of course, I wouldn't show anything of my recognition. I remained "calm" and "delighted".

"Child abuse, women's suicide, and untested medicaments are what he wants me to know; in order for you to know everything already, he didn't want me to say anything further to each complaint," I explained as we had been sitting there for a while and chattered for lightening the mood. No faked surprise or any viewable change of expression did the accused show, but his sons eyes widened, and he looked almost furious towards his father, scared of what these judgmental facts would mean for them.

"Very creative; even throw I don't at all see what this has to do with the complained industry." His voice was friendly, warm, and not at all like we were talking about such judges. Another fact that made me know that it wouldn't surprise him, since it was true, Now, it was just about showing me how powerful he is as a person to make me feel better.

"The judges against your industry, you already know, even throw that the medicamentation well belongs to it." I didn't stop to smile calmly, like he did too. For an extern, our conversation may even seem like an exchange between old friends or good acquaintances, even if we neither had seen each other nor any friendly prospect with this conversation.

"I think that there is not much for me to argue, since these statements are going to be said anyways at the court. We can just stay strong against that together." His polite smile almost became wickedly for me. Together was the friendly world of unneutrality.

Tacking a side wasn't allowed in any case for me, even if this one, with personal influence in my private life, already had a little bit of this. Of course, the parliament wouldn't get to know that; in the end, I didn't want to lose this case, which had such a strong meaning in the public eye. Already, the last cases had been popular, even if they just ended with an unacceptance of the penalty, which led to an upgrade of the case. Over and over again until they reached the Supreme Court. This would be the final and last judge, with a concluding punishment or complaint. Never had anybody had the option to take the risk and push it as far as that. It meant much to everybody who had ever been confronted with the events of the pharmaceutical industry's largest ambivalence of being responsible for creating medicaments to save human lives while making money with them.

"If there isn't anything further," I said, raising an eyebrow while I looked at him, waiting for an answer. It wasn't really in my interest to stay anywhere longer than necessary, since it would just waste our time.

As I took on my jacket, I recognised a letter in it. Nathaniel Favouner looked at me with a knowing smile. "I am glad to have you as the president in this case, Maxwell." He pronounced my name slowly, and I recognised a shiver of danger in me. With a friendly smile, I nodded and left the house. I hated people who thought that they could solve everything with their money. On the other side, I didn't have anything against taking it. Even if my job is well-paid, in a few years in pension I would may need it. Therefore, it was better to have more rather than too little of it. Additionally, my neutrality in this case does not exist.

On the way back, I got a call in my car. The number was familiar, from deputy president, which was used to get the information for the earlier cases, since that wasn't anything I liked, but in this case, I already knew a lot.

"Hallo Martin, have you found a lot already?" I asked kindly, even if "already" was more of a joke in itself. If I had done that, I may have needed a day, not more than two. He had been on this case since the middle of last week. However, his research never had any mistakes, and he would also take several calls to get advice on how to treat the primary cause.

"Yes, I finished the last call right before I called you. They all said pretty much the same, and the information is very similar." He explained what I already knew. We went on tiny stones, with burning lava beneath it, in this case. That was our job, but on the other hand, it also dominated a lot of our private lives.

"The cases ended all with losing it all together or getting a refund as a payment if patients or their relatives had it. Complaints had been the high pricing, unfunctional medication, and lack of transparency about where the substances are from," he explained, and I nodded to each statement. Apart from the primary cases and large issues, there were many others too.

"However, Maxwell, be careful. They all warned me that they were important to our society. Yes, they may have made some mistakes with the medication, and you know, they haven't been perfect, but still... He didn't find the right words for a while. "We can't lose them, so don't hang yourself up too much into this. In the end, we aren't going to change anything about it," he explained his fear, but I didn't want to make this case end like all the others. Whatever was in my power, I would find the best information I could. Neutrality had never existed anywhere.

Chapter 3

The importance of remaining neutral didn't seem to be important for everybody. Some even took jobs, even if they knew that they were influenced by past events but didn't show or say anything about it. The hope of changing anything remained inside them. It had been made very clearly in my studies, which I finished last summer, that whatever case it is and how much we need the money or want to be apart of it to expand our knowledge of our names, we can't take it as once we are influenced. That wouldn't be for our country; that would break its rules and neutrality in judging.

Luckily, it was part of my job to point out colleagues who may have been affected somehow. Even whose I "worked for," the President, I had made a check upon. His wife died of cancer several years ago, but he didn't seem to judge the pharmaceutical industry for it. Which was good, but made me still wonder a little, since the reason for her death had been that the medication didn't work. They had already said that everything was well after she took plenty of chemotherapy, but while she took the medicine, it increased again. Later, they figured out that it was faked and didn't have any active ingredients in it at all.

However, he had assured me that it had been a long time since then and that it was only humans who made mistakes. Additionally, without their help, she wouldn't have lived at all at that time, he had been saying. I took it as a warning: don't bother with trying to find any influence in me; I am as neutral as anybody could be in this case. Since it has been hard enough to find many people who are not related to it, while the pharma industry is the largest and the one that we all will need once in a lifetime, With the afterthought of our relatives or our own health, it's hard to judge them.

On the other hand, I had made many calls to experts on this issue. They had all warned me not to remain neutral and be for them. I had been saying that it wasn't my job to choose a side, but that I would keep it in mind for the later case. Not that there was much danger with going against them in such a case, but the fact that they also, aside from many not functioning, had delivered good medication, which had helped many people. May I need it someday, too? My wife is pregnant; if she has any complications, it might be smart not to go against whoever may help her.

My next station was the paper house, as I called it, which was just the place where the journalists wrote for the papers. The fact that the house was white and, because of the windows on each side, almost looked like an opened book, gave it the name paper house. My wife always used to laugh at that, as she too wanted to work here once before she got pregnant. May they offer her a job afterwards since she really is as neutral as I am? Which would make her a better journalist than many others who are writing today.

My last visit for today was with Juliet Hardstyle, who had been the correspondent journalist in this case. I hadn't been reading them, and since there wasn't anything interesting in the case before, I got it, I thought it was best to talk to her in person. Neither had I checked her background, which I usually would do for safety reasons, nor, of course, the neutrality of the person. Sometimes it could be hard to point out the facts or beliefs, and then somebody would take anything aside. However, I believed in my professional observing sense to remark this.

"Hello, Mrs. Hardstyle." I reached out my hand, and she shook it with a polite smile immediately. "Hello, Mr. Devenson, right?" she made sure herself, and I nodded politely. "What can I help you with today?" she continued politely, offering me a seat. "Thank you; I wanted to get to know more about the explosion of the clinic, which you'd been writing about," I explained, and her face went pale at once. She nodded with a faked smile and sat down herself while she stopped looking at me at all. "Yes, exactly; it has been a long time since then, but I do remember everything still," she assured me with a smile, even if I remarked with a little unsureness about what she would say.

"If the time doesn't fit today, it would be fine to do it on another day too. The case is," She cut me off, which, well, wasn't polite at all. "I know, I know... Well, I" she didn't find the right words and stammered, unsure of what to say. "I am persuading you, since I surely am going to write about it again," she figured out, and I nodded sceptically. That was a little too much unsureness and not finding the right words for me to believe that her issue was completely true.

"However, what exactly do you want to know, Mr. Devenson?" She looked into my eyes with a smile again. I tried to remain as polite as always; even if the dismissal of her manners was very clear, I had to get some facts before I would leave.

"The exact events that have happened and every other knowledge you may have about why they would think about the favourite . pharmaceuticals as a reason for that it happened," I didn't miss eye contact with her, therefore I saw a little relief and more comfort in her as her smile increased.

"Of course," she said, standing up to get some papers for me to show.

"This had been the article in the papers, with a picture before the explosion. However, I do have some right afterwards too, if you want to see." I nodded, not asking why she would have some "right after the explosion".

"That is incredible," my eyes widened at the sight of the pictures. The entire building was destroyed. You just saw parts of the cellar— even some dead or injured bodies in the background—but the rest was just a mess.

"Why do they..." I stopped myself from asking if they wouldn't think that it was a bomb, since I didn't know that many of the medical devices could explode like that.

"Why would they do that? That's a good question, but since it happened after a patient's death, it might have been uncertain in general at this time," she explained another question, clearly taking aside that it had been their guilt.

"In your article, you write from both sides, even if you're clearly supporting the pharmaceutical." I wanted her to explain, but as I said that, I saw her jaw tense.

"At first, as you mentioned, I tried to take in both sides. However, since Mr. Favouner didn't want to give me an interview, I could just put in what I knew from the other side," she explained, but she didn't show me the message she might have sent him since it was deleted, like she said. Even if I had heard that they wouldn't remove any important chats until at least the case was finished.

"You're saying that you don't have any connections to the other side through?" I asked since the pictures, sources, and text all together seemed to be a little influenced. After I said this, she wasn't only tensed, but I recognised that she also tried to maximise the space she took in the room.

"Well, nothing further then that my father is working for the Favouner's," she explained, and I frowned. It was a little confusing that they both had the same names, but that wasn't the reason for my wonder. Since it was quite obvious which of them she meant.

"They let you write this article, even if they know that you may be influenced by your father's job." I tried to make my concern clear, and after a bit of mumbling, she agreed. Was that the journalism of this century? Power took over rather than knowledge or the ability to write a neutral text.

"On last question, before I have to end this conversation, since you can't give me any further neutral information's," I pointed out and wondered if it was smart to remark that she should make it notable that she's influenced or taking aside on her next articles if she doesn't want to miss her job because of having a case against herself with that.

"Is there any possibility that your father could be one of the victims in the case since he, as a worker, knows the events that are happening in that clinic and may be more neutral since it is just a job for him?" I asked her, keeping in mind that they didn't have anyone until now.

"If you're thinking that this will help, I could surely ask him. On the other side, have in mind the risk he would take by losing such an income and job at his age." She was impressively concerned about having a neutral judge in the case. However, even if she was right, it would sound better for them to have more victims than just their lawyer and the accused owner.

"That doesn't matter. Say to him that it may even show everything more positive if they do have more victims for confirming or declining the complaints," I explained to her, and she nodded in silence. As we didn't have anything further to say, I stood up to leave.

"Mr. Johnson," she called out after me, which made me turn around at once, wondering if she wanted to give me even more information or what else might have gotten into her mind.

"Thank you for hearing what I've got to say, but please don't report that my last article wasn't neutral. I assure you that I am going to change it or remark on it in my next texts." Her eyes were clearly begging for it; however, I just nodded and left without another comment. In the end, it wasn't my fault that she would do anything alike, nor was I responsible for the neutrality of something that didn't belong to my colleagues or my job's most important issue.

In the car, I took a call to the president to inform him about the information I had gotten. He answered as always, shortly and politely. I knew that he wasn't satisfied with the tempo of my work; however, I hadn't worked for a long time, which meant that I didn't have as strong a routine as he had. Additionally, I was more certain of where I got my sources from, which was used to make a clear background check. I excluded the conversation at the end of the conversation with Juliet Hardstyle today. An expectation, nothing more than that. I thought, as I arrived at the house of my wife, that, for some reason, the ambulance was already waiting.

Chapter 4

"They are surely going to let us inside soon," I tried to assure Deen, even if I didn't know anything about it. Never had I been in any kind of judge before.

"We aren't going to get to enter before the audience gets to come in. Maybe we're going to be the first, but that doesn't include that it isn't going to take half an hour more." He was obviously not pleased with the fact that we had been waiting an hour until they let Nathaniel enter, and now fifteen minutes later, we stood there still outside in the cold November air. They are running late, but we couldn't change anything about that or do anything else, rather than wait more.

"What about getting some food on the other side of the road? I am starving," he explained, and I felt the same since we both hadn't been eating anything since breakfast.

Five minutes later, we stood in the same place again with a sandwich in our hands. Despite the two men who had entered the building at the end of the day, I hadn't seen anybody else. However, that did just support the uncertainty, but it wasn't my true worry. I just wanted to know when it started and what would happen. Additionally, I wondered about the result in the end, but that was a long way from that. Deen already warned me that such large judges could stretch themselves out for further days. Unbearable ones, there we would stay here overnight since it wasn't of any sense to make the hour's drive furth and back every day.

Another ten minutes passed, and with each second, I could see that Deen got more nervous. His clinic had been open for some weeks, and I could tell that he didn't like the fact of not being there for his patients. Technically, they wouldn't need any doctors. However, that didn't matter for him. He owned it and therefore had much other work to do, despite being there for his clients.

Finally, the doors opened, and they let us in. We went inside at first and took a seat on the side where Nathaniel would sit. Until now, nobody of the judges had appeared, but they told me that this was usual and that they would come, and then the room was filled with people who wanted to join us.

"Deen, Lusie" Nathaniel turned around and whispered our names so that we could barely hear them. We showed him that we both listened, and he continued, "We can be lucky to have a public forum today at all. The president of the judge today put his job at risk with that, since it wasn't fair or usual that the public couldn't be apart from such large judges. Otherwise, the pharmacist would have declined it. You should have seen their faces," he explained, explaining why it did take such a long time before we could enter. Until now, I could just guess why they didn't want any other people inside here. Later, it would get even clearer.

The room itself wasn't very special. In front of us was a small podium, which the highest positions would sit on today. The rest of the room was very similarly structured; each of the accused and complainants sat at the front on each side with their lawyer. The next row there are the relatives, or closest to the case in general. In this case, me and Deen are behind Nathaniel. Behind us sat some journalists, and after them was the public, which did want to join today's case. Altogether, more people than I had imagined, surely further hundreds.

Deen took out of the blue my cold hand in his warm. I looked at first surprised towards him, but as he turned to me with a gentle smile on his lips, my body lost twenty-five elephants of weight, which my sole had been bearing the past days.

The older man, whom I had seen earlier today, entered the room at first. After him followed the younger one and some unfamiliar faces. "What is going to happen now?" I asked Deen while whispering in his ear. "Stand up. Now," he ordered me, and I recognised that the rest of the room was already standing.

We remained standing until they sat themselves down. Firstly, he would answer, "It's a symbol out of respect and politeness for their authorities. The first thing that is going to happen is that the president makes justice, which means that he explains again what the judges from today are against and from," he whispered to me, and I nodded silently while watching what would happen in front of me.

The so-called president began, which is the older man who had given us the pity look at the entrance.

"Today's sake, from Doctor Nathaniel Favouner, former owner of the PVT cancrocum clinic. Against Doctor Nathaniel Favouner," I already heard some people whispering to each other as they heard that they both shared the same names. If they only knew...

"Owner of the Fav. Pharmaceutics, one of our largest pharmaceutical industries in the country," he looked up for a short second, more to the public than anybody else. Even if it seemed like he was searching for anybody.

"We are going to make a special expectation of the case today and divide it in two: one against Mr. Favouner himself and the other against his industry," he explained, and I frowned. That had

Nathaniel never said anything about. Neither did I know if he appreciated it. He hadn't mentioned anything about wanting revenge on his producer—just the truth about his industry for the people to know.

"If we start with the complaints against the industry," he said, taking a deep breath before taking the large list into his hands while corrugating his glasses so that he could read it better.

"The high drug prices themselves, which have been judged by other patients and affected people before, Additionally, the questionable marketing practices, which are judged for including off-label promotion of drugs, misleading advertising, and undue influence on healthcare professionals to prescribe their products and pay each of the doctors differently," he explained, and the chatter got louder in the background, which made just him talking even louder, so that still everybody could hear him clearly and understand for today's sake.

"Also, drug safety concerns, which still pose risks to patients, Drug recalls, safety alerts, and adverse events have raised concerns about the safety of certain medications and the adequacy of regulatory oversight. In addition to that, the medication hasn't been tested at all or too little sometimes." The chatter got louder until they had to wait for a while until the room calmed a bit at the astonishing facts.

"We've also had the familiar complaints of the lack of transparency within the pharmaceutical industry, such as undisclosed conflicts of interest, hidden clinical trial data, opaque pricing structures, and the fact that they wouldn't give out any information ever about where the medication is from." Now they all remained silent, already too shocked to complain with anything or say another word to the facts that stood in the air of the room. The atmosphere was rare, but even more awful was the fact to see the man, who didn't even seem a little tensed while they spoke out loud the destroying facts about his industry. Nathaniel didn't even seem to look at him. The similarities in their look and size made my stomach rumble and hurt painfully. They had never seen each other before, and neither did they share any personality traits, but still, it was rare to see them as close as on each side of the room.

"The Intellectual Property Rights Act heavily relies on patents to protect their innovations and recoup research and development costs. This system is said to hinder competition, limit access to affordable generics, and perpetuate monopolistic practices, which leads well to some of the above-named facts." He frowned and swallowed deeply before he continued with the next fact, which almost seemed to affect him personally.

"Overprescribing and Overuse, since the pressure to meet sales targets and maximise profits has led to concerns about overprescribing and overuse of medications, contributing to the rise of antibiotic resistance, opioid addiction, and other public health crises, as for example, the lack of active ingredients." Deen suddenly took my hand again, which comforted me more. With each point, it became more and more clear to me how important the sake really had been, not only for us but for everybody. It was now clearer than ever before for me why Nathaniel had been trying so hard to work without any influence from them.

"Health Inequality. Disparities in access to healthcare and medications, both within countries and globally, exacerbate health inequalities and limit the ability of underserved populations to obtain essential treatments. Which earlier deals with them from our country actually did assure, but the industry didn't fulfil," which was one of the reasons why we had gotten to achieve such a high instance. Since it did affect everybody, the entire country and world suffered from different sicknesses.

"The last point is political influence. The pharmaceutical industry wields significant political influence through lobbying, campaign contributions, and other forms of advocacy. Critics argue that this influence can undermine public health priorities and impede efforts to implement effective regulation and reform. Which makes them not neutral anymore. Related to the last fact, makes it them controlling where they want to send their medications too, or even choosing these without active ingredients," he took a sip of water that stood on their table before he stated the other again.

"Against Nathaniel Favouner in person are sakes as child abuse, at a private brothel, the women's there hold against their will and visit each day without good intentions and not enough health care nor food to have a good living." Now they started to whisper again as loudly that you would have to scream to the person beside you, else they wouldn't understand a word. The judge clearly got angry and begged for silence if nobody wanted to leave the room. With the knowledge that the accused wanted neither the public nor journalists in here at all, I wondered if it was this that he had hoped would happen and begged that it wouldn't because of that.

"Also, he has discriminated against women in general; a named fact here is the sending away of a woman because she had forgotten to take birth control. Since she didn't own or have anything, she had to start as a prostitute as her only possibility, which later also affected the children's lives." Nobody dared to say anything anymore, but what I clearly saw was the change of expression on his producer, who now stared at Nathaniel in shock.

Even if I thought that he'd known it before, now he's aware of what they meant. It surprised me that Nathaniel had named the fact in front of everybody at all. Earlier, he didn't even want anybody to know his name, but now, as he didn't have a chance to leave the situation as it was anyway, he took everything that he had against him without taking care of his own privacy anymore. That had been the reason he lived for, because of, and against.

"Additionally, the harming of whose in both psychical and physical ways," he swallowed deeply, while my mind travelled back in time as he had been sitting in front of me, saying that until I wasn't married in his house, I was available for everybody who wanted me. This looks on my clothed body, like I would stand there as an object he wanted to buy. How vulnerable, naked, and scared I had been...

"As the other facts are also strongly connected to him, as the owner of the industry, I only have one last fact against him as a person." We all looked at the president, and even the accused Nathaniel Favouner started to look more interested in the last fact; rather, he'd almost seemed bored with the past ones. Which almost was wicked itself, since it was about child abuse, violence, and mistreating women's, which he well didn't have anything for or even didn't see as humans at all.

"Spying, blackmailing, and, in the end, bombing the clinic, which caused the deaths of the workers at the PVT clinic on this day," he said, along with the date, place, and more exact dates. This was the event that many people thought was our reason for being here. Most of them didn't know that it had been stated much earlier and that the majority of instances had already been done while the clinic was still in operation. It was almost sad that, to the last fact, which had been the most damaging for the people themselves, didn't anybody react at all either. There is no news anymore, but it wasn't provable, unfortunately. However, Deen and I had taken up many calls and saved messages from them, which had strong indices. That had to help. We must win this case!

Chapter 5

"How long are we going to have time until they start this again?" I asked the brothers, as the court had already laid in a pause.

"Not longer than two hours, I think," Deen answered, while Nathaniel Literary was just present in person, and his mind surely was still at the court.

I took his hand in mine, which was now warmed up by Deen. He swallowed deeply and looked down at me.

"You're doing fine," I tried to assure him, since the named facts at the start of the court had already been very much for him compared to how the public reacted too.

"We'll see about that," he squeezed my hand, and together we walked to the nearby café to get something to eat for lunch.

Outside, the wind was hissing through the small gates. People tried to get their way home before it soon started to rain. Nobody had any idea what was going on inside the courthouse today. They are all there heading after their own ideas, struggles, and vain. With their own families and friends in mind, maybe business too for some of them. The people who passed them didn't matter, as long as they all fit into their world picture. An expectation that everybody should meet. If that weren't the case, it might not be that easy to just pass them by without looking at who they were. Without wondering or asking yourself where the person was headed or why they would look like they did. Normal meant unrecognisable in the city's, which already had forgotten how to have hour-long conversations with a stranger. Unfamiliar faces never mattered as long as they followed the roles and fit into the small gates, like they always had.

"You shocked him with the part about Coco," I said while we waited for our food to come, and Deen smiled, amused at the thought of the older man's pale face with wide eyes.

"He knew it already, I think. May it be just that I named it in front of everybody, since, you know, I haven't even said my name to anybody in the past years, despite the two of you." Natheniel seemed to relax a little while we were there alone, talking about the court, instead of continuing it. Additionally, it wouldn't be smart to start a conversation about anything else since our minds still proceeded with what had happened and were not ready for distraction already.

"Did you know that they split the case in two?" Deen asked, and he sighted while he leaned a little forward, making sure that nobody else but the two of us would hear him.

"They told me it before the court; they did it since it isn't possible to judge the pharmaceutical industry for an individual act of one person, even if I assured him that I was neither one nor one person, but that all close workers had been there before. Even if we have it on tone, it may not be enough, but the employees surely wouldn't say anything about it anyways, since they make themselves guilty then too." Nathaniel explained that issue to us, and I started to wonder if they really had only been talking about it before the case started. Also, did Nathaniel's already meet and talk behind the scenes?

"Well, but that's the Supreme Court. I was already impressed that we have access to it. Even if it affects the entire country, we aren't going to change any laws or regulations." Deen explained, and I recognised the firm, educated voice he had, not like the playful, charming man he always had been. How could such a short time already change him that much?

"They haven't said that much about it to me either. I just accept it as it is and trust in their knowledge about what rights they have to exercise. In the end, the pharmacist is not unimportant either.

Nathaniel stopped to talk as soon as the service came with our food. Politely, we all thanked her, but I remarked that Deen didn't look after her like he would have done before with every blond, long-legged beauty legend. He remained looking at Nathaniel and me instead, seemingly concentrated on processing the information about the past events at the court. Even if I wondered if he might also think about his clinic.

"Do you have to talk with him?" I asked Nathaniel, maybe a little out of the blue, but we all knew exactly who I meant and why I asked.

"I don't have it, but I am surely going to soon. It's not like I try to hide from him; since I am here at the safest place I've been to for years too, I would almost appreciate him starting a conversation with me. There is not much that could harm me in the end," his calm voice told me. He'd been thinking about this too much. Already considered different topics that his producer may want to have a conversation about with him and is not at all afraid to face them. Even if I had seen that, he seemed a little stressed as he saw him that close in the court. It could also have been because of the court itself, but somehow, I doubted that since he'd prepared himself for it for years. Maybe more closely in the past month, but still, I couldn't imagine that taking him away from his calm mood.

We started to eat, and silence surrounded us for a while. Even Deen didn't say anything. Usually, he'd always been the one who wouldn't tolerate such things at all. Now, it didn't appear like he'd have any problem with it at all. The only louds I heard in that moment were the rain, which had started a few minutes ago, and the chatter of the other people who sat inside the restaurant.

"Excuse me," an older woman said beside us. Almost out of nothing. At least I hadn't recognised her before she stood right beside us.

"Aren't you this Nathaniel Favouner at the court?" She asked, and the irony that she could mean both sides made me smirk. It wasn't that precise to remember just the name in that case here, even if it was clearly what she meant.

"I am," Nathaniel said calmly, and I recognised that it had been the second time now that another person, despite being one of our trio, called him by his first name. The first person in public, but that would surely change now altogether. Soon, every newsletter would print this case on its front page. This case he had lived for was not just literary, but it was also going to change his life completely once it was over.

"Very good. Well done, with the case. I really appreciate that finally anybody took that much offence to start this. It had been really necessary," she praised him while she tried to catch another chair behind her so that she could sit down beside us.

"I don't want to interfere with your conversation more than necessary, but I still have a very important question to ask," she smiled carefully while everybody looked at her in silence.

"My husband was diagnosed with lung cancer last week. We really wondered if you would start your clinic again after the case, or, well, excuse my mistake, build another one?" She corrected her sentence since it wasn't possible to start anything anew that didn't exist anymore.

"Even if I don't know the stadium of your husband's cancer, I can say that it might take too long to wait for it, even if I start to build up a clinic as soon as the case is finished," he started to give her exactly the advice she could do without pharmaceutical influence. She was very delighted to get his help, even if she seemed to be disappointed that he couldn't treat him himself.

"Thank you very much. I really appreciate it that you took the time. I wish you the best of luck in your case, even if you're going to win it anyway. At least that's what everybody thinks. The facts you've figured out about that person and their industry are just too harmful to even think about. However, I am very sure that you're going to have good evidence material to prove everything." She smiled and nodded towards us again before she went away. I started to wonder at once if people really thought that we had such an easy game to play for the case to finish. In the end, I had hoped for it. Additionally, it was almost impossible that anything else would be said, since it would also make the public furious. In the end, we would see what they decided. The time until then was just unbearable. In a week, we'll all be smarter and know what we've done wrong and right. Just whose seven days, one-hundred and sixty-eight hours had to be waited.

While we finished eating after the woman was gone, I got a little curious about how everything would continue from now on. The start of it had been like the content list in a book. Not at all like I had expected. On the other hand, I hadn't been there before, and my only ideas there were made out of my fantasy. That all together would last for several days was still a mystery to me. However, with the thought that they had needed such a long time just for it to start and took almost the same length of breaks afterwards, it became more clearly and obvious that it would take a very long time until we got finished.

"When should we head back?" I asked as I thought that we had some time, but not forever, for lunch. We had to be there some minutes before the case continued again, since they didn't appreciate late arrivals at all.

"In some minutes, but we don't have to stress until now. We still do have time," Nathaniel assured me, and I leaned back again. Trying to relax, which was already hard enough for me, is surely impossible for Nathaniel, who even here hides his emotions most of the time. Well, we are there in public attention now anyways everywhere, but still. On the edge of this small café, it didn't seem like many people were watching us. However, maybe it was the best for me too, since it wouldn't really calm me to see how much Nathaniel feared losing the court of his life.

"I would just go now," Deen said and stood up, looking back at us as we didn't.

"May it be smart to go to the toilet before the afternoon session?" he pointed out understandingly, and we both stood up and followed him. Not hand in hand in public, but still as close as I could feel his body warmth, which comforted me so much. Hopefully this will stay forever, including after this final court in the next few days.

Chapter 6

"Would you like to explain to me what this was, Mr. President?" Johnson wanted to start a conversation about everything as soon as we were back in the other room.

As I didn't respond but ignored his pleading for an explanation, he continued.

"Mr. Sterling, you promised me to be neutral; otherwise, I would have kept care of not involving you in this case. If you would explain this accident to me, Now," his demanding voice made me smirk. Right from the school bank and already gotten too many rights here...

"Mr. Johnson, I would appreciate you listening to what I said and had to do rather than wasting my break with this nonsense." My voice was calm and collected, and the fact that he was inches tinier than me made me look down at him. Maybe even literary, as I really didn't appreciate young people who tried to take over a world that they didn't know anything about. Thinking that they are the best and know everything better than all the generations before them.

"I ignore this accusation, since I've been calling you, my friend. However, what happened right now at this court was neither agreeable, neutral, nor beneficial for them; if that's what you wanted to reach with that," his voice got smaller from the anger that flooded him. Years of accusations, fights, and conflicts had made me calm even by such a reaction. I knew what I wanted, who I was, what I owned, and which position I had here. Compared to all that, he was nothing. Right at the start of getting somewhere. For doing so, he had to take off these rosa glasses to see what the real world looked like.

"I don't beg for any ignorance of the facts I have named. Nothing more has I done. If these are appearing negative for you, it might be because they aren't any positive; if you may have considered this fact," I turned around. I wanted to take my jacket for a walk outside, but when I heard the voice behind me, I knew that I could forget about that at once.

"Mr. Johnson and Mr. Sterling are in one case. What a pleasure" the judge came towards us. I even used to call him "the judge" in private. We used to play golf together each month, but since he'd joined a larger club, I didn't go with him anymore. I enjoyed myself alone too. Not like him, who needed people to come along with his life. Other humans meant other opinions, which often led to conflicts. For that, I'd grown too old. Silence was what had become the highest quality for me now.

"Justice Benjamin Wright" I said his name like I had heard it the first day today at the court. He looked rarely at me, but then laughed like I'd made a joke about it. I. did. Not a joke, ever.

"It must be a very touching case for you; I wondered that you wanted to be apart of it." He took his hand on my shoulder, like he still cared about what had happened. The hidden message behind his words was that you shouldn't be here; it isn't good that he's trusted you. Still, you are weak. Even if it was so many years ago, you let your private life become part of your job here right now. Something I don't appreciate.

My body tensed under the hand, which touched me. It had been some months since I saw him last, and he had aged again. Being in his late fifties, he looked more like seventy. The lack of his earlier black hair didn't make it better. However, he also had enough stress, which surely made him stay awake some nights. With a daughter who committed suicide in the eighth grade and a son who later started using drugs, he wasn't an example of an easy life either.

"We are talking about the incident at the court right now," Johnson explained to show his importance while he stretched out his body a little more, for being at least not inches but only an inch tinier than me.

"Incident?" Wright raised an eyebrow at him, and I hid a smile. Even if it had been years, he would surely still define us as friends. Right now, his protection was amusing to me because Johnson's face would turn white as snow at once. I was unsure what he should say against that now.

"It wasn't anything of importance, just that I thought he may sound a little too affected by everything." It wasn't long until you could call it stammering, what left his mouth. He was uncertain, intimidated, and scared to lose his position, which he had gotten. He knew that nobody would cry about that, despite him, if that happened. Not that he didn't do his job, but the way he did it in, after exactly everything that they had gotten to know at their law school. That wasn't the way we acted here. Of course we had blind people, like the judge himself, here, but many had understood that our system wasn't as good as its façade. Not officially, but behind the scenes, nobody would decline to get a bit of money for doing this or saying that. Orientating themselves on other, already succeeded countries, or, as I would say, being afraid of a worse call, therefore doing everything to not be kicked out of the warm pot until it's too hot and burns our asses.

"I see." Wright looked at Johnson from head to toe, like he scanned him for any mistakes in himself.

"If it wasn't of much importance, I would need to talk with the president myself." Johnson understood the call, nodded, and went away so hastily that it looked normal. I remained there, looking after my dear deputy president for this case. Hopefully he would get fired soon, or at least recognise himself that this wasn't the right place for him. A tiny nemo-fish in between the sharks would never have a good ending otherwise.

"You wouldn't mention the paragraphs, as you explained the curse of the court. Therefore, it sounded like you, an unknown judge, judged yourself. Let us figure them out together. Like before, then I came as a newcomer into this position." His voice was gentle and calm, but it was exactly these voices that made me shudder.

Faked. It's too easy to accept and tell anything that they definitely shouldn't know.

"I will do it myself and repeat them in the case once again," I said calmly, and he shrugged a little, disappointed. Seemingly. Faked. As always.

"If you think that this is the best way, hold yourself maybe a little shorter now; I have to get my son afterwards," which meant as much as just saying the paragraphs and what they stand for, not a word more about that, since I have to get my druggy from the surely thirty withdrawals he has been on.

Kindly, I nodded. "Of course, we will end today's sessions as soon as possible." We smiled and nodded politely towards each other before he went away again. Finally. Now I could work in **silence alone**.

After about an hour, I was finished. Of course, I had prepared myself earlier and wrote down all the paragraphs that were important or could be relevant in this case. Now, I hadn't eaten anything. My stomach rumbled, but the court would start in just a few minutes. Perfect.

Hastily, I reached for my beg, for which I always had some food inside, if the time wasn't enough to reach any store until the court started again. I ate the energy bars fast before the others had already stood up and made themselves ready for going out into the official court area again. So, I did too. While we went out, everybody stood again. This was something that would never change. Impoliteness everywhere but in court.

After everybody had a seat, the rest of the public would do that. First, after the room was filled with the comforting silence again, I could start with the paragraphs and a short description of why these would relate to this case exactly.

"We start with the first paragraph, related to the high drug prices." I said the paragraph and then continued with what Wright had told me not to do.

"The pharmaceutical company found guilty of engaging in price gouging or unjustifiably inflating the prices of life-saving medications shall be subject to fines proportional to the extent of the price increase, with a portion of the fines allocated to subsidising the cost of medications for disadvantaged populations. Repeat offenders face suspension or revocation of their licence to manufacture and distribute pharmaceutical products." I didn't look at Wright, but I felt his gaze burning in my skin.

"The next is the paragraph." I named it where it stood and what it was called, like we'd learned in law school. At least Johnson would be satisfied with that. "About the Drug Safety Concerns. The pharmaceutical company must adhere to stringent safety regulations governing the testing, manufacturing, and distribution of medications. Failure to comply with safety standards, leading to significant risks to patient health, shall result in the immediate recall of the affected products and the imposition of fines. Additionally, companies may be required to fund independent investigations into the safety of their products and implement corrective measures to prevent future harm." Which leads us to the next paragraph and what it stands for.

"Transparency Lack. The pharmaceutical company is obligated to maintain transparency in their operations, including disclosing all relevant financial interests, clinical trial data, pricing methodologies, and any potential conflicts of interest. Failure to provide accurate and comprehensive information to regulatory authorities and the public shall result in penalties, including fines and public disclosure of non-compliance." A brief look into the publicum told me that half of them were bored, while the other ones noted themselves the paragraph and in what way it was connected to the case. Even if I didn't want to please Wright or Johnson, I didn't want to lose them. I had to speed up a little more.

The paragraph about intellectual property rights was the next one;

"The importance of intellectual property rights in fostering innovation is that pharmaceutical companies must balance these rights with the public interest in access to affordable medications. Companies found to abuse their patents or engage in anti-competitive practices, such as blocking the entry of generic alternatives or engaging in evergreening tactics, shall be subject to regulatory intervention, including compulsory licencing and fines for anti-competitive behaviour."

Next paragraph and what it was about. Even if I had to be careful not to talk too fast so that everybody would understand me well, it was surely fine not to talk like a bear in hibernation.

"It is about overprescribing and overusing. Healthcare professionals must exercise caution and prudence in prescribing medications, ensuring that they are used appropriately and in accordance with clinical guidelines. Pharmaceutical companies found to incentivize overprescribing through marketing tactics or misleading advertising shall face sanctions, including restrictions on promotional activities and mandatory education programmes for healthcare providers on appropriate prescribing practices." Somehow, further people listened as they knew that I would have come to an end soon.

Paragraph about "Health Inequality. Which measures shall be implemented to address health inequality and ensure equitable access to healthcare and medications for all segments of the population? This may include government subsidies for essential medications, expansion of healthcare coverage, investment in underserved communities, and targeted interventions to address disparities in healthcare outcomes. Pharmaceutical companies found to exacerbate health inequality through discriminatory pricing or distribution practices shall be held accountable and may face penalties."

"The last section for today, related to the industry itself, is about the political influence." After I'd named the paragraph itself, I told them briefly about its course and reason.

"Regulations shall be enacted to limit the undue influence of the pharmaceutical company on government policies and decision-making processes. This may include restrictions on political contributions, transparency requirements for lobbying activities, and mechanisms to prevent conflicts of interest among policymakers. Any attempts by pharmaceutical companies to unduly influence legislation or regulatory decisions shall be subject to scrutiny and may result in legal sanctions, including fines and restrictions on lobbying activities." My voice almost went dry, so I would take a sip of water before starting with just his cases. The reason I parted with it was mainly the warning that it wouldn't be possible to judge the industry for all this. Additionally, it shortened everything a little. At least the process.

"Found guilty of child abuse, including physical, sexual, emotional, or neglectful acts against children, shall face severe penalties, including imprisonment, fines, and mandatory participation in rehabilitation programs. Child protection agencies shall be empowered to investigate reports of abuse, remove children from dangerous environments, and provide support services to victims and their families. Perpetrators may also be subject to lifelong restrictions on contact with children and registration on offender databases, according to the paragraph. "After I've said it, the tenseness in the air was there again. Until now, everybody had ignored it, but this was at least one of the most shocking facts for all of them.

"Discrimination against women, including unequal treatment in employment, education, healthcare, and other areas, shall be prohibited and subject to legal sanctions. Employers, educational institutions, and service providers found to engage in discriminatory practices shall face penalties, including fines, loss of accreditation or licensing, and court-ordered remedies to address the harm caused. Victims of discrimination shall have the right to pursue legal recourse and seek compensation for damages, which is according to the paragraph." I got a little more fluent with that. It is unfortunate that we only had four of them left.

"Individuals who cause physical or psychological harm to others through acts of violence, coercion, manipulation, or abuse shall be held accountable under the law. Assault, harassment, stalking, and other forms of abusive behaviour shall be punishable offences, with penalties ranging from fines and restraining orders to imprisonment, depending on the severity of the harm inflicted. Victims shall have access to support services, including counselling and legal assistance, to aid in their recovery and pursuit of justice."

After I had said the paragraphs for the next one too, I took a brief look into the publicum again. It always astonished me that they needed the drama so much. A case about that anybody had a token a child's favourite cuddle toy interested nobody. May it have been just me who suffered more for children's pain than for adults?

"Unauthorised surveillance, espionage, or spying on individuals or organisations shall be prohibited and subject to legal consequences. Spying activities conducted by government agencies, private corporations, or individuals without proper authorization or legal justification shall be considered violations of privacy rights and punishable offenses. Perpetrators may face criminal charges, civil lawsuits, and regulatory sanctions for their actions, including fines, injunctions, and loss of licensure or accreditation. Which is said in the paragraph, I named it "as illegal," may that sound more "neutral".

"Blackmailing, extortion, or coercion of individuals or entities through threats, intimidation, or the dissemination of sensitive information shall be unlawful and subject to prosecution. Perpetrators shall be held accountable for their actions and may face imprisonment, fines, and civil liability for damages inflicted on victims. Victims of blackmail shall be entitled to legal protection, including restraining orders, injunctions, and compensation for any harm suffered as a result of the blackmail attempt."

"Now we come to the last one about the acts of terrorism, including bombings targeting public or private facilities, related to paragraph," I said, referring to all of those I had found. Which there are altogether five. "Shall be treated as heinous crimes against humanity and subject to the harshest penalties under the law. Perpetrators of terrorist acts shall be pursued, apprehended, and prosecuted to the fullest extent of the law, with no statute of limitations for their crimes. Those found guilty of terrorism-related offenses, including murder, shall face life imprisonment or the death penalty, depending on the jurisdiction, and their assets shall be seized to compensate victims and their families for their losses. Additionally, measures shall be implemented to strengthen security protocols, enhance intelligence gathering capabilities, and prevent future acts of terrorism through collaboration between law enforcement agencies, intelligence services, and international partners." As I was finished, the court was that too. For the entire rest of the day, like Wright had wished.

Chapter 7

With every step we took away from the courthouse, I felt that my body relaxed in a way, like our mood altogether. Even if I hadn't recognised that I had been so strained the entire time, it felt good to come away. That it didn't just explain my feelings, but for all three of us, made that we came into a comfortable conversation while I was holding both of the brothers' hands in my favourite place, the middle in-between them.

"Already hungry again, or shall we start to do anything else before we get some food?" Nathaniel asked easily, contrasting the man he'd been within the judge; he was tensed and collected, and even if he didn't show it, I could tell he was frightened too. That all of them seemingly spoke positively for us may have taken some weight off his shoulders now.

"What about heading to the hotel first and doing anything afterwards?" Deen suggested, and it surprised me again and again how fast a person could change in such a short time. He was still the same, I said to myself over and over again, but something told me that he wasn't. Changes don't have to be negative. Neither do they have to destroy relationships, since positivity is a matter of opinion. I wondered how the people had done that before—married maybe already at the age of eighteen and stayed together their entire lives. Both of the partners changed throughout the years, but they still remained a couple. In the end, they were just two and did have it easier than us with three, but still, I don't want to imagine the number of fights they had. To this time, you even hadn't, or with many struggles afterwards, the right to divorce yourself from a man.

Well, I didn't think about marriage until now since it seemed to be fast-paced. Even if I hadn't planned to leave any of the brothers', bind yourself seemed more like an issue they had for years ago. Old-fashioned. Still, I saw the idea of having a beautiful lifetime together, but never had I heard that marrying that person would help anything more than maybe getting some more possibilities after an incident or another curse of death for one of the partners.

As we came to the hotel, it looked surprisingly normal. Not like the five-star stuff he'd been ordering for us before. Imagine that I had already grown tired of having to be careful to say a word because the entire area was silent. Businessmen's and company owners had a break that they wanted to share in silence in a hotel, which they paid well for. Me wanting to have a good time with the brothers', imagine that this also concluded a conversation and not just silence. Hopefully, at least the walls there are wholesome and isolated.

We entered the room, and I broke out in laughter at once. He even tried to order a room for three, which meant that we had a normal double bed and another, which I might fit in if we rewind the time five years, and I wasn't that tall. Maybe 5.5 feet, or anything alike, at least not like my male company, which was much taller than me.

"I suggest you sleep in there." Deen pointed to the miniature bed while he spoke to Nathaniel. We laughed as he tried to lay himself down in it. It was just his upper body that fit in; the legs stayed outside. However, he is really tall; it would surely be better if I took it if we had to do so. On the other hand, I could already see us in the double bed together. At least I hoped for that. I wanted to be in their middle all the time if I had the choice. Being with one of them was great but having them both was unexplainable and much better.

"Why did you even try to book a bedroom for three people? You know that they just have this bullshit." I laughed while he raised himself again and had to stretch out from the limitation of space he had gotten into.

"Tell me what I should have said at the reception: the room for two persons; don't look at the blondie; he is just our fast company-pet." Nathaniel smiled while he said that but started to laugh at once as I looked into Deen's shocked face.

"Company-pet?" He repeated the words in amusement and shock with a raised eyebrow. I couldn't hold myself, and neither did I try. We all laughed, but the nickname was given, at least for the rest of the day.

We came to an attraction called the best of the city. Maybe it was the culture I didn't understand or know, but somehow it seemed to me more like a half-collapsed building than something I would have wanted to see. Broken dreams, lives and hearts may be within it, but such a long time ago, you could pass every building in Rome and think the same. On the other hand, maybe my comparison to the most beautiful place I had ever been was a little unfair.

"Dog or cat?" Nathaniel asked without any signs of humour, seemingly. The truth was, well, just that he would never show any kind of mood in public.

"Do I look like a cat? Rather a pit bull terrier," he said easily too, but I had to start to laugh at the comparison between him and a fighting dog. Even if he had gotten into some conflicts before, he had changed into a grown, educated, and solid man who had started his own clinic under the age of thirty. This may have included fighting too, but that wouldn't make me say that he had any tracks to this dog race, neither externally nor internally.

"What about you, Lu? You seam to me like a Norwegian forest cat," Deen teased me, but now it wasn't me that showed any affection, but Nathaniel, who smirked. That meant much to the public about his mood.

Without any further comments, Nathaniel took out his mobile phone, as he may have figured out that I'd never seen such a cat before.

"The Norwegian Forest Cat's fur is medium long with a woolly undercoat and water-repellent outer hair made of long, shiny guard hairs." He read the text he'd found somewhere about the description of the outer look of this race and looked at me while he considered how much that fitted me.

"A long ruff," he said, raising his eyebrows, "knickerbockers and tufts of fur between his toes." His eyes widened with "shock," and his attention turned to me again. "Take off these shoes, Lusie; we have to check out that." I laughed and shook my head while Deen tried to capture me, but I ran away before he had the chance. It may have looked childish, but it was one of the most beautiful things that could have happened on such a stressful day.

In the end, he had me, of course. Even if I had been a good athlete at school, I hadn't had any training or chance, since two of my steps meant one of his. As he had me in his hands, the mood changed. Amusement, laughter, and a simple joke were gone. He stood behind me, his hands holding me on my hips and pressing me lightly towards him. His head lent itself to me so that his breath touched my skin, like the warmth of his body. My mouth opened immediately at the string impact his nearness had on me. His eyes fixed on me while he looked into mine. Before I could tell what was happening, his lips touched me at first gently, but then deeper in obvious want and desire. Weeks had gone by; I'd seen him only late in the evening, then he was exhausted, and we all just went to bed.

Weeks had passed, but still, our affection was the same. If not even more after such a long time without any touches for both of us. Our bodies have longed for each other, and the flame between us burned brighter than ever before.

Luckily, we were there alone at that place. Nobody would go to this "attraction"; maybe it was just a joke that we didn't get on the internet. However, the fact that we were all there alone in public didn't change the fact that we still had to behave ourselves. At least

I realised that as we both stopped breathless while Nathaniel stood beside us with a gentle smile on his lips. Immediately I wondered what he felt; jealousy wasn't common for him. Being happy for us is more likely. On the other side, I wondered if he wanted to do that too. Being easy around people and viewing any kind of affection may not have been easy for him. Still, he could have this desire, which he might always have, but never show or act alike to satisfy it somehow.

"I am sure we'll have the chance to continue everything in the hotel, but what about getting out of public and maybe catching some food before that?" he suggested, and with the word "we" stinging between us, we went to that restaurant together. I wondered what he was thinking and if Deen would like or appreciate it, since he was the most vanilla or" normal" of us. At least he had always been that afraid of what his desire could lead him into. On the other hand, he had changed, obviously. Which could mean that he may not only be more comfortable with himself but also with the desire that burned inside him. I felt that the next few days would be otherwise; we would still have the case, but that only made us even closer and with more energy inside us, which we had to use somehow. The question was just how we would do that.

Chapter 8

Sometimes I asked myself if time existed. At least it couldn't go at the same tempo, even if I knew that it did. Before the case, I had weeks to prepare myself, but those weeks felt more like a few days. On the first day, I wouldn't have to say a word at the court itself since everything was formally introduced for the public, press, and state to understand. I imagined them registering every single word that had been said and planning every single detail that had to be done on which days. Today was just an introduction for everybody to suit themselves so that they would be prepared for tomorrow.

"I wonder how long it will take before we are going to repeat the restaurants we visited," Lusie said while we got our meals at the Vietnamese.

"Before that, we are going to find us another place or home, so that I can cook for us myself again. If not Deen, who had been engaged with the preparations of breakfast that much, wants to try that by himself," he almost swallowed and began to cough. I patted on his back until he had calmed himself, while I smiled.

"I wasn't supposed to kill you already," I said in amusement. Lusie had gotten tensed at once; he didn't get to eat properly, but smiled her sunny angel smile after he had taken a sip of water and breathed normally again.

"What about if I would help you, like you had been doing with Jake?" she offered, while Deen sat down in his class again, shackling his head while he figured out what to say to her. It was months ago, but we all remembered the rare event of having Deen in the kitchen with Jake each morning, preparing breakfast for us. He seemed to like it back then, which made me wonder if it was since he did it with Jake, not the event himself. Everything that man did, he could make into a power game. While Deen always tried to refuse and ignore it, he was still interested in the submissive side, which I could imagine that he had to show while they had been cooking together. "Policy for our host, that had it been. Nothing else," Deen said while unsurely taking the cutlery into his hands again.

"Don't come back to your already little brother." It was seldom that I used to say anything like a family-connecting word to call him out. Before we'd done it more often, at least he. Now, it was over anyway. I had done it the hard way—first, at court, the public would know my entire name at once.

He didn't say anything, and neither did he start to eat. At first, he looked down at the table, processing the few words I had said, before he laid the cutlery down in its place again.

"Next Friday" He started to raise his voice, demanding and sure of what he wanted to say. Not like months ago, he would minimise himself to not draw any negative attention. People learned that this just worked for a part of time, never forever if he wanted to reach anything. Still, it had almost surprised me how fast he had changed that.

"Next Friday, we are going to that café again. Meeting whose people," his words there were not filled with any emotions, nor did he show them on his face. I knew that he might still be afraid of the largest step he had to take for his own pleasure and desire. The acceptance. It had been the longest way for him, even if he had the most sexual contact with others convinced by us. However, sexuality wasn't anything that mattered while being open to other sexualities. BDSM I sometimes almost wanted to convince myself that being homosexual means you have to accept it before you can enjoy it. Even if my thought was that we are all bisexual, I would accept if some people insisted on being heterosexual. This would show me just again and again that we are still a long way before everybody can be in love with whoever they want to be. Since we never really accepted anything before, we felt it by ourselves, but as long as they declined it that strongly, nobody would feel what they could by not desperately declining everything that had been illegal centuries ago and still is in some countries. The acceptance was, for all of us, the first step in modernization.

"I am in." I smiled knowingly, knowing that Lusie would die for getting to that meeting. We had to skip the last ones since neither I nor Deen had time to get to them anyway. Now, as we were all here anyway, we could just help Deen with everything he had to do with his clinic before we headed to the café together. I could imagine it being even better.

"Hopefully the case isn't going to last that long," Lusie said carefully, not wanting to affect my mood by not being pleased with sitting there for so many days. I could understand it. Especially on the first day, where I hadn't gotten any sleep the night before, I had almost fallen asleep while they complained over and over again. Not everybody understood it after they had been saying it the first time. No. They had to make it more clear which paragraphs each complaint involved. Some of them had even further ones; even if they mentioned the punishment for some of them, I had to remain neutral, even if a glimmer of hope started to grow in me.

"Maybe two days, not more than that. We could help Deen out on Friday, so that we could drive to the café together at fore p.m." I had already created my plans exactly for how long before the start we had to start to drive to the place to when we could head back to get something good to eat at a restaurant. I had noted to myself that time we were there visiting the place.

We head back to the hotel, which showed me again the unusualness of not being a couple but a trio. It didn't even have to be another double bed, which I wanted, but just not a 5'3" x 6'6" bed, which sometimes could get small for two people. Not that I had any problem with holding Lusie in my arms throughout the night to capture less space, but I could tell that this would lead to a discussion of which of us had the "right" to do that that night. Poly was good, but it involved a lot of talking to make everybody satisfied with our system or any other relationship that functioned that way.

"Someone who wants to join me for a shower?" Lusie asked, and even if I didn't have the attention to do that, I wouldn't have been able to say a word either.

"I am in." Deen said fast, so that I wouldn't take "his space," and I entered the bathroom with her. I sat myself down at the window and looked at the plan the president had given me hastily today after the end of the case. It noted everything that would happen tomorrow, with exact times noted for each event. We had to register who we would like to have as a judge for us, but it was still possible that they wanted to hear or had already informed other people to get further points of view there.

Case from Doctor Nathaniel Favouner against the Fav. Pharmaceutics and Doctor Nathaniel Favouner (head of that industry)

Plan for day two of the court;

Start 9 am: Clarify criminal liability for witnesses'

9:30 am: First hearings of plaintiff and defendant

Break at 10:30 am

11:00 am: hearing Gloria Devenson

Break at 12 am

1 pm: hearing Deen Miller

<2 pm: hearings of the accused, with witness Greg Hardstyle, and complains

President

Maxwell Sterling

I didn't know if it was usual to receive such a plan, but maybe he'd noticed how nervous it had made me not to know what the past day would lead me into. I was almost waiting to be called out every time anybody started to talk, but I never heard that I should do so too or say anything at all. Like that, it had ended; my first day at court was solved without any word of what I had to say to each of the facts.

It took Literary almost an hour for them to finish their "shower." By the time I saw them smirk as they exited, I could tell what had happened in there. Immediately, I tensed, but I reminded myself that the operation had made it possible for her to have penetrative sex again. Nothing else mattered to me. As long as she was well, I was fine. The same applied for Deen, since he was important for both her and me.

Chapter 9

Who did he think he was? First taking my money in his wrinkled hands, and already on the first day at court, taking aside for the others. That wasn't what I had paid him for, nor was there anything smart to do for him. Everything you did against me, you would get to feel by yourself, and I wasn't patient. Especially with him, but also elsewhere. Never.

"He doesn't have a wife?!" I shouted at Henry for the first time in his life. He was supposed to find anything—just anything that mattered to the old man.

"Favourite car, house, hobbies, or maybe an affair?" I wasn't used to being so angry at not receiving what I wanted. The majority of people knew that it wouldn't be smart to kid around with me. He did that too. Which made it even more hilarious that he did this at court. Maybe you were not saying anything directly, but sometimes it was just the way you said it. I had remained calm and didn't show a hint of affection as I sat there and listened to every complaint my name-bearer had against me. Another fact that made me hysterical was that even if I had made fun of calling him "my son" to that slut he had on his side while I tried to get some facts out of her, I never accepted or thought about it anymore. May it be the only time anything shocked me yesterday. To hear the words aloud in front of everybody. May not directly, but still for everybody with a brain to realize. I was the plaintiff's father.

"Dad, he really hasn't done anything." I cut him off, at first for trying to calm me by calling me such words, and secondly for not being anything better than he was and not finding **any kind of** information. It hadn't to be the wife or pet that I would let suffer, since for a man who had nothing left, already simple things mattered a lot. It appeared to me that he belonged to this sort of human, which would make me destroy him at once. He missed this one thing he still held onto.

"Can't you trust me? He doesn't own anything; he just rents apartments or hotels and plays golf in his free time. He doesn't have much of a life already now." The fact that he appeared to have pity for that fucker who had tried to ruin my surface at this court didn't make anything better.

"Make him loose that fucking position, if it is his job that he holds onto," my voice cut through the air, and I could only tell that they would do the same or even worse on the other side of the line.

"That would be too obvious." I hung up before he could finish his sentence. My father had taught me how to receive my will. Now, I would get everything I wanted. At once, if it doesn't want to suffer for letting me wait more than a second.

I would stay at a hotel that was closest to the courthouse. It wouldn't make sense to drive back and forth each day, even if it would be better to at least have my wife here, if I couldn't take a better snack with myself. However, as I ordered room service, it was the polite woman who got me my dinner, which received some "pleasure". I took her by surprise as I asked her to check out if the bed was broken or what that sound on it was. Whatever was wrong with that cheap stuff, she could hear the sound herself at once she bowed down to look at it, I bend her over and fixed her tiny arms, so that she wasn't able to move anymore.

A dry pussy was better than nothing at all. Even if I wasn't enjoying it that much, it was still acceptable enough for just a day. Her yelling I stopped with pressing a pillow on her face. Even if it might have been more enjoyable to feel the short tightness of her tiny pussy as the last breath leaves her mouth, it would be too obvious, so I had to keep care of that she caught some breaths. We got it still to work two times successively; even if I was in better form than that at home, I took care of that; she didn't work for me either and had other customers anywhere at the hotel. They may have wanted anything else, but that wouldn't stop me from taking what I wanted.

The next day started at nine a.m. at the courthouse. It was a fitting time for me to rest properly before I had to hear about this stuff again while having an expression of nothing on myself. At least I would surely get to say my suggestion today; if not, my lawyer would have resisted doing that himself.

Today there were hearings. My "dear" son was already there and had taken a seat with his lawyer and accompanies, who were surely going to play their part at the court today.

I should have noticed it at once. Why I had believed that blond man, who sat right behind him, was surely because he had mated himself criminally while staying with me. Out of purpose, I had given him, the sixteen-year-old, something against him. That I would have to use it that soon wasn't in my purpose, but since they wanted and almost begged for it, I didn't have any other options.

As the justice came in, I stood up with the rest of the room. Maybe one of the things I hated most was being insulted.

Polite, formal, and seemingly calm while cooking more than a burning pot of fire. That was my skill, which I didn't use that often since I enjoyed playing my games more than hiding my emotions. Changing what's beneath the beautiful surface of reality has been my passion and reason to live, well, forever.

"The court today against Doctor Nathaniel Favouner and his industry, Fav. Pharmaceutics, accused of Doctor Nathaniel Favouner, former owner of the PVT clinic cancrocum, is held by Justice Benjamin Wright. "They started, and I sat formally there, not looking anywhere but at them. That had been my acting yesterday—desperately trying to figure out if we had any similarities at all. In the end, he was my genetic son, if the whore of my wife hadn't betrayed me while she lived in my house, which I didn't believe.

"Before we are going to start with the hearings, I want to make sure that the witnesses know that they are going to be judged if they make false statements." He pointed out the paragraphs and punishments you could get for that, and I wondered how they would ever get to know if somebody did that. In the end, their system too was very contrasting to what they said. At first, they didn't want anybody to make false statements, but on the other side, they bribe people with less time in prison by making reports of events that they never could have seen. Many criminals would do that, even if it involved the betrayal of a friend. On the other hand, what was a friend in the criminal world? Maybe as much as my friends are there for me. Business companies, whose you believed most and the only people you could say what you really there doing, by sticking a knife into their back as once they aren't trusty enough anymore. Or even better, ruining their lives, which would intimidate them so much that they wouldn't dare say a word anymore.

"We start with the accusations for Doctor Nathaniel Favouner" that they even bothered with saying the name like that would point out anything more.

"Discriminating women's, harming them in both psychical and physical ways, we will have a witness in this case too, but before we please her to tell us her story and the events she had to experience, I would like to let the accused start to defend himself." The worst was that I wouldn't know what I would say against that. My father had taught me how much a woman was worth to my own mother. He was a very dominating man, and I am compared to him as very kind to the other gender. At least I did let them do anything other than housework and serve men's. Coco wouldn't have been alive anymore in his hands. He would never have paid for all the operations to keep her acceptable.

My lawyer stood up as he recognised that they were talking to us and cleared his throat before he started to say, what may be the smartest thing to say since well, every woman who had met me could be used as a witness. I included this brown-haired slut beside the blond doctor, who had betrayed me.

"My client admits he is not guilty of any crime. We do not consider any suggestions to be true," he said firmly, and in a way, he was even a little right since I didn't do anything wrong. In the end, our society made the largest mistake of giving way to women after their power wishes. If they just stood still, the world wouldn't have changed to become such a rare and awful place.

Gloria Devenson. That is her name now. She'd changed it, even if I wouldn't remember what it had been for maybe twenty years ago. She wasn't anything special. I was just one of many girls who lived in my brothel. She may be a little stubborn sometimes, but not as stubborn as others.

"I lived at his private brothel for several years and got apart from his daily visits like the five other women who had been there to that time". Since then, I have upgraded the brothel to get almost twice as many women into the building.

"Lucky me got pregnant from him and wasn't usable anymore. Since I didn't want to die of the way of the abortions, which already many women before me had to suffer from, I ran away on my eighteenth birthday." As the public noticed that she had been that young at the time she was there, they all inhaled in shock. Whatever they thought, if they imagined it to be a cheap hobby, they were definitely wrong. The prizes had increased more for every slut I bought in the past few years. At least it appeared to me like that. Maybe it was just the uncontrolled market that made them adjust the payment after my salary. I didn't know, but in the end, it was still worth it to buy a tiny new cunt instead of using the others, which were partly already cracked after several games I'd played with them.

"Was there never any other chance you could take for running away?" The president asked her kindly, and his warm-heartedness made me almost roll my eyes. She did have it that bad. They got food, a roof over their heads, and all their basic needs satisfied. I wasn't a monster either.

"I tried," her words echoed throughout the room. All the eyes were fixed on her aged body.

"They caught me the first time. After that, I was so-called free-wild for a month, which meant that he would have business meetings at the brothel and seemingly invite everybody to abuse me. With whatever they wanted, how long they wanted, and with whatever damage it made," nobody said a single word anymore. All the eyes are on me. The monster, bastard, or paedophile, as they might think. Nobody saw me as her safer, which I am. There are worse people outside there. Everywhere. She was lucky that I bought her and nobody else. We had fun. She had everything she needed. That she ran away wasn't my guilt, just hers.

Chapter 10

I recognised that I had even stopped breathing. The room was filled with such silence that I heard my heart beating. Throughout, everybody looked at the man who had done this to her; my eyes weren't able to look at him after that at all. He had been kind to me. Even if his words were still in my ears to make me shiver, my belly wrangled as I recognised that I felt almost sick.

"You know the rules, Deen. Until she isn't married, she is free for all of us." the freedom I had longed for while staying there, which I figured out to be a contrast to it.

Now my breathing is increased. Still, nobody had said anything. Deen took my hand, but I wasn't even able to comfort him a little. My thoughts went back to his villa, the place where I recognised who he was and what women were there for him.

As I looked up again, I recognised that the president had his eyes on me. Hopefully my reaction didn't seem any wrong, like I had anything to do with this. It was unbearable for me to imagine that a simple human being could hurt others that much just for its own desire and satisfaction. If I knew that I would do that by myself in any way, I would rather live as a celibate than harm anybody else for my pleasure.

"Thank you, Gloria Devenson. We're going to take an hour's break now," the president informed us, as nobody else would speak. Maybe it wasn't a minute altogether, but it felt like hours; that much harm, damage, and shock had run through me while I tried to put myself in her position now. She had never looked at the man who did that to her. She wouldn't have been able to say a word if that were the case. I wondered what effect he still had on her and if she had been able to process such events over time. In the end, she had built up a large security company, but still, it was more than possible that she just did that much to burry her emotions into the hard work. Never showing them. Getting used to living behind a façade. She never tried to think back on the events, even if they haunted her every single night, which never gave her any rest.

"Lusie" Deen was already standing beside me. I looked up at him, at first not understanding what was going on. Break. The rest of the room empty. He wanted to go anywhere.

"Why wouldn't he accompany us?" I asked as we were there on the way to find a place to eat. Nathaniel had been staying inside, or even went into the other room, where the judge had disappeared all the time, after the president had asked him something.

"He will be there later again. They just had to discuss something organisational, I think, since the pharmacists followed them." My body tensed and shivered in horror at the thought of them being in one room. Maybe only some feet's away from each other. Maybe even talking with each other... I stopped myself at the last thought.

Nathaniel wouldn't change for somebody he hated as much as anything else. He knew what he was doing and chose every step carefully. Always, I hoped.

"Did you know about that earlier?" I asked Deen as we sat outside in the sun at a small café.

"How should I have known about it? I may have been inside there before, but at these times, nobody had served any punishment like that. Luckily," he said, and I realised that he too hadn't had any power over what he could do inside there. Everything was controlled by the pharmacist. If he hadn't obeyed, I wondered if we both wouldn't be alive anymore.

"We're going to be the next at the judge." Deen pointed this out, but I shocked my head knowing that I wouldn't have to speak in front of all whose people.

"You are; they don't have any benefit of having me there," since I didn't imagine that I wanted to stand there and be even closer to the other side, nor that I would be able to say all that I'd seen in front of him while he could stand up and hurt me at any time. He probably wouldn't, since he wasn't that stupid either to do such in front of everybody. It would just confirm his personality, which the entire room had stared at. Heartless. Power-sick. Coldblooded.

"I understand that you don't want to, even if you wouldn't be the best witness they could get for the primary time. May you haven't been to the brothel or labours, but this isn't about anything else but how you felt about being there. How he discriminated against women's and harmed them in both psychical and physical ways," he pointed out what the judge had been saying at the start of everything. Even if the pharmacist never got to lay a hand on me, his manipulative suppression of me I still felt in my veins. Hate, which was seldom for me to feel. Never had I hated my mother. I never hated Eliza, but he was another thing. What the pharmacist did didn't just hurt me. It was the frequent worry and nightmare reason for many women every single day. Some might even wake up and find themselves in the nightmare still. I was hopeless that it would ever end.

We didn't talk. Both were deep in their thoughts. We ate in silence until half an hour had passed and we figured out that it would be best to head back again. It wasn't smart at all to do that, and then the masses tried to get through the doors. Therefore, we were there about ten minutes before the court would continue. The thought of that made me already shiver. I hated it to be here. Even if it was the final step to an end, they couldn't let him go. Something said to me that he would never change his primary point of view and just continue to harm innocent women until the end of his disgusting life.

"We are continuing with the witness, Doctor Deen Miller. Who has worked at the PVT clinic to that time but visited Doctor Nathaniel Favouner for several weeks," the president introduced, but before Deen could even get on his place, other people's words echoed throughout the room.

"Objection. He wasn't visiting. He was spying," the lawyer of the pharmacists said to defend his client. It seemed like a bad point to make, since the next thing we would talk about was them doing such to us.

"Objection not accepted, please start Dr. Miller," the judge said at one cooly, and I could tell that he wasn't a person to kid around with. May he held himself neutral and the state rules in mind, but still, it seemed like he was not that unbased, like he tried to pretend to be.

"Fow talking about the discrimination and harm in both psychical and physical ways of women, I would like to start at the brothel and how it is structured now." Deen told them about everything. The look of the place and where it was. How many women served there, and what exactly did they have to do? Still, it wasn't enough for them. They would send the police out to that place, but they wanted more information. More about how he acted in general towards women.

"Mrs. Lusie Amans, I know that you aren't a planned witness today, but still, I would want to hear your point of view as a woman, since you stood with Doc Miller at this place at that time." I already felt all the eyes on me as he pointed out my name and person while he looked at me. Deen nodded with a smile toward me. Trying to comfort me by saying what I'd seen. If I would do it, it would be for nobody else but Nathaniel. His case. Past and hopefully the final end of it forever afterwards.

"My first greeting was the scanning of my body. The search was to see if I was good enough for Deen. Love doesn't exist there anyways, I figured out very soon. He also warned that he should marry me as soon as possible, since until then, I was what Mrs. Devenson ad pointed out as free wild, in his house." A short inhalation of shock flooded throughout the publicum. Something they had with this word, I figured out. May they have read anything alike before or seen such in any movie? This they could picture out in front of them, which meant that it harmed them most.

"In the kitchen I was sent to in the end, after they blackmailed Deen about what they would do, he wouldn't let me go away. There I got to know his wife and one of his daughters." In the second I said that, I saw two familiar faces in the publicum. Sitting the longest away, trying to hide them from being seen. Coco and Abigail. The pharmacist didn't know that they were there; I could tell. If that had been the reason, they would have sat behind him or become the best witness imaginable.

"They told me about what he'd done to them, in both psychical and physical ways," I pointed out, while the thought that they were there comforted me a lot. Out of danger. Save. Maybe this is the first time in years. Still, it wouldn't be smart to look at them and point out their presence. Otherwise, they might get into danger in the end here too.

"Both of them had to go to plastic surgery, especially the young Abigail. Just for him to accept his own flesh and blood. If they wouldn't obey..." I inhaled sharply, remembering the wounds I had seen hidden under a lot of make-up and the hint of synthetics that they wore.

"If they wouldn't obey, they would get punishments, as not getting food for a long time, not having the right to get outside, getting slapped or beaten by him was well one of the harmless punishments since the act itself didn't last that long. Still, the scars I had seen. They would never grow, at least in a woman's heart at such a place. At least the nightmare would haunt them for the rest of their lives every single night until the day they die." I tried to make it viewable and feelable. It was surely impossible to imagine the entire situation for anybody who had never felt such harm to themselves. It was easy; it said that it was over, then it was finished. Maybe that was also like that for some people. However, the most I know and have talked to suffered until the end of their days of such. Forever hurting. Never forgetting. Waking up each night with the same fear; being there again, found and bound to the old life.

"Thank you, Miss Adams. We're going to continue with the other accusations for now. We'll make a final judge of everything at the end of the cases," the president explained calmly, and I went to my place again. Hopefully it would have helped them, I thought and wished. I couldn't do more for anybody. That was all I knew, aside from the details Nathaniel had told me. These are better to hear out of his mouth here, but they are not that important to me anymore. I just wanted to get away from seeing this man and have him set into prison for the rest of his poor-soled life.

Chapter 11

"Doctor Nathaniel Favouner, finally I meet you in person." The thought that nothing could still make me shiver in horror disappeared at once. This voice, with the following knowledge I had about him, his industry, and all whose it competed with—all this together made the worst killer in the world look like an innocent lamb. He was even one of the worst, considering that he just didn't kill directly. The only thing he wanted was the money to make people's symptoms better. Healing wasn't something they wanted. Ever.

I turned after a while slowly around. Not bothering to haste for that empty-eyed sole. As we were almost on the same high, I didn't get the pleasure to look down at him, which I had with the most people. However, the idea that he was my real father was the worst ever. Even if I had never considered anybody as my parent, if I had to choose, I would definitely take Deen's instead. There was no question or dwell on that.

"Or should I call you **my son?**" he pointed out as he was closer to me, and I had not fully turned towards him. Like, that was a name I would react better to. Just in the want of intimidation, suppression, and the realisation that he had his fingers everywhere, Even if the court itself hadn't looked like it went positive for him, right now nobody has stopped him. By now, he could have taken a knife out of his pocket and killed me. Nobody would be close enough to stop him, but maybe there wasn't anybody who would do that either. In the end, the largest problem they would have is the public, which knows about the case. Even if they could just continue with it without me and tear everything down, the judge wouldn't be that much in the end anyway. If I would die, that was the contrast to what I wanted to reach with that.

"Remember your words as you blackmailed her to leave you thirty years ago; if you still have that in your mind, I am dwelling on the fact that this type of description of us wouldn't be right," I clarified by using all too many words. It showed myself that I didn't want to have that or any other conversation with him since I wasn't comfortable in any way. May words meant just the reduction of my brain's capacity, which usually would figure out how to say everything in the shortest, most collected, precisest, and most direct way to avoid any misunderstandings. If that wasn't the case, as it also sometimes had been with Lusie, I got influenced by anything.

"If I don't remember a thing, I may still have it in mind this day, but also the day of her return," he reminded me that I wasn't existing in his world. The day of her return meant the day when she said to him that she didn't have any children and excused herself from his place.

"Impressive that she didn't dare to say the truth to somebody like you." It wasn't meant to sound that much like I looked down on him, but still, it did. My desire was to end this conversation, not to give him more information about what he may have imagined about our relationship. I wondered if it was the same hate we had for each other. They shared the same blood. Did that mean that we also had the same feelings? I hated that idea. I didn't appreciate anything that was connected with him. Even if he hadn't any choice or didn't take his side, It was just something in my mind that struggled with the thought of "his.".

"Impressive that you still dare to go to judge with the past unfortunate events that had damaged that small clinic of yours." I wasn't a psychopath; that was maybe the biggest difference between us. He did care about others feelings, just for the manipulative reasons. That he thought that he could play such games with me made me almost smile in amusement. I suppressed it still, knowing that to laugh about him wouldn't make the situation any better.

"Just for giving you a small hint of information," he said, stepping closer to me, and I had to fight against the urge to step back at once. My body tensed, my fist balled, and my heartbeat increased. He was lucky that I had such self-control; otherwise, else that might not end well for him.

"They haven't found anything at the house your little fake brother mentioned. Not even my DNA. As we share parts of that, I would like you to not destroy my name, which includes not being that naïve that you imagine winning that game. If you were a real man, like I would have taught you if you had grown up at my place, you would deal with that by yourself. Talk to me instead of sending whoever you love most. Can you imagine how much information I got out of them? I have to just push a tiny button to destroy them and their lives at once. That you didn't come to me was a step that just showed me how frightened you are, since you're smart enough to know that you'll never win anything. I give you a tip on what's right to do if you want any change." His long monologue whispered into my ear was worse than a diagnosis of a soon death. It disgusted me that he stood there, so close and still seemingly calm. The only thing that told me that he was not, was the long talk about what I should do. Did he really believe that I would ever trust or do what he said?

"Stop the case and go to my house to talk to me yourself. Not like a shy child, letting anybody talk for you. If you were a real man, at least then you would do so," he pointed out the inexistence of my maleness in his eyes. If he were what he described as a man, I would rather be a cat or anything else, despite that. I would have laughed at his belief that I would like to become like him if he hadn't meant it that seriously. Additionally, it wasn't smart to laugh at a man like him. May he even laugh or smile too, while he, in the same second, pushed the button he had pointed out to harm me in the most perverse way imaginable. Since he knew that torturing me wasn't helpful, as long as I knew that everybody who was under my protection was fine, He was stupid enough to start that conversation, but he wasn't that foolish that he would let me win this "game" easily. That would be too much for him. Additionally, not only him and his call, but everything that was connected to it. It didn't even matter for him what happened to him as long as his industry went on forever. Another type of torture for me.

"Doctor Favouner and..." the deputy judge stopped to call out after us as he saw that we were standing that close to each other while he finally finished his years-long monologue. At once, the pharmacist turned around to face the young man. While he did that, he hit my hand. With purpose, I could tell as soon as I felt a small letter inside of it as he stood beside me.

"We wanted to inform you both that we would continue with the rest of the cases, including the witness speech of Mr. Hardstyle now. Tomorrow is our plan of ending everything with the final judge," he pointed out, and I swallowed deeply at the thought that I knew about my life's importance in twenty-four hours. I wondered if I had done anything against that industry. Even if it would be a shame for the state if they tried to get through it, while the entire public doesn't want them anymore, just to still have them as a large part of their BIP, People could sometimes be naïve, but if it could be that bad... I couldn't tell... Surely they would all choose his side in panic as they get any diagnosis that they think is not healable. It was always the sickness and pain that drove us to take decisions we did not want to make.

"If you're ready, we would just continue now," he pointed out, as nobody of us had answered. There was no question. No need to respond; still, in that moment, I felt like I had done anything wrong. That was exactly what the pharmacist wanted to reach. The judge didn't know what he had been saying to me. They just saw us standing there while he whispered anything into my ear. If they are smart enough to see our relationship and who he is, they would surely figure that out easily by themselves, but I am dwelling on the fact that they want to do that in any way. They just see and hear what they want to, rather than what really is the case, like it is with people in general.

"We're continuing with the complaints of spying, blackmailing, and, in the end, bombing the clinic, which caused the deaths of the workers," the judge pointed out, as it was the most known complaint in this case. Some people who sat in the public area might even have lost their husbands at the event. For the public itself, it was perhaps the most damaging of all named crimes, even if it was the one that hurt fewer people than all the others. Relating to that, it was just me, maybe Lusie and Deen, but else the workers and their families, not hundreds of women and children who worked for him in any way, nor all the patients who saw the medicamentation as their last help, even if it was the first step to death.

They gave the word to us at first: "After the recognition of many people in the surroundings and inside the clinic who didn't belong in it, but also patients who worked for the Fav. pharmaceuticals, we placed cameras and made our security more aware of whose facts." My lawyer pointed out the facts and took on the videos and pictures we had taken on the large screen. On them, you saw people sneaking into the clinic, taking pictures of the medication, making a call, and already starting with saying his name. It was the worst thing to do in an unknown place as a spy, but however, it gave me clear proofs, so I wouldn't blame them. That Richard Gardiner, the former leader of youth welfare, which had given me to Deen's family as a child, was a part of it was the most shocking fact for me. I had treated him for his cancer for months and even talked to him more than many other patients, but still, he would do that behind my back. I wondered if he had felt any guilt or if the money, he had gotten was enough to prove the good side of his mind about death.

"Additionally, calls there taking, for example, Deen Miller was blackmailed to give them the information they wanted if he didn't want to see both Doctor Favouner and Lusie's deaths after a long torture. If you want me to take the records, I can do that, but I want to inform you that the content might be too intense for parts of the publicum," he pointed politely out to the judge, who said that he should rather send it to them if he doesn't think that it belongs in court right now.

"The explosion itself," every whisper that might have been before was silent now, and all the ears listened to his words, which might be the reason that many people did come to the court at all.

"The explosion is the result of the fact that we didn't obey the constant warnings of what would happen if the clinic didn't stop by itself," he pointed out, but the judge didn't see that as enough evidence to make such an accusation.

"As the police and others didn't find anything at the place, we didn't make us the way ourselves, since it still isn't sure that there was anything explosive left." Deep sights of disappointment from the publicum started before he continued.

"The only fact I would like to reveal again, this time here at the court with the pictures as proofs, is that there was nothing explosive in the clinic itself. All the devices, even if they are not able to cause such damage, were taken out of the clinic before the construction started." He showed them the pictures I had, just in case anything would get stolen or changed while we were there. If they were not enough, I couldn't tell what it was.

"Thank you, Mr. Morgan. I would like to hear the other side's explanation of how such videos could be taken, and if there might be any connection to the explosion itself," the judge still dwelled upon the fact, even if I myself started to wonder what they wanted. A video of the pharmacist pressing the button before everything explodes into a thousand pieces, like in any kind of action movie? I hope that they knew that this wasn't doable to make as long as you didn't have any connection with anyone who had been doing that by yourself.

"There are no proofs at all that my client has anything to do with this event. Neither is there any evidence of a connection to the others, since it's only the easiest way to think that there is any connection to the first person you think about, while there are many others left who do have the same name or might use it as a code or synonym to harm Doctor Nathaniel Favouner themselves. Not to mention that it might have been themselves that made the videos for this case an illegal kind of preparation for proving all of wrong," he said, firm with an accusation he probably shouldn't have made since it already sounded stupid by hearing it the first time. Since why would I bomb my clinic, ask diagnosed people connected to them for acting as a spy, and in the end pay for all the damage myself? I have been obsessed with that case for many years, but never have I been a psychopath who just wants to prove everybody wrong. Yes, it had dominated the largest part of my worries, not only for the past few years but for my entire life. Still, I wasn't stupid enough to play an illegal game just to get them into prison while I had other facts that would do that by themselves alone.

"I assume since you aren't showing any proofs from your side, that you haven't any either?" the judge asked, a little sceptical of his statement.

"Since we aren't playing any of such "games" ourselves, we don't monitor everything to make such videos. Additionally, it would have been more of a crime to make that on a place we don't own, which makes your request of a proof obviously to a question of if we have done that and made other kinds of videos to prepare everything to prove the other side wrong at the case," he tried to explain in a complicated way, which showed me the struggle he had to find the right words. May it be even as good as it was, in the way he argued, it would be foolish for the judge to give them right. I had the public on my side by now, as the older woman had explained, and as long as they would be against it, the judge themselves couldn't make anything with the fact that I got what I wanted—for them to dwell about the pharmaceutical industry altogether, even if we hadn't even started with the accusations against them.

Chapter 12

Everything seemed to turn out well, and I already saw the hope shimmering in my brother's eyes. The accused desperately tried to come away from all the proofs and complaints, but what they really did was struggle with the right words, which made it sound like they didn't have anything at all to say, which was right. It seemed like the public had been taken aside; even if they didn't have the right to do so, the justice system didn't seem neutral anymore. However, I didn't let myself hope for a positive end until my ears told me that tomorrow.

Lusie was a hundred percent concentrated on catching every detail herself. I was sure that there was still a lot that she hadn't heard before, since I knew my brother—he would try to protect her by just saying necessary events and nothing that would make her nervous or scare her off.

For a lot of the time, I wanted to suit and comfort her by just holding her tiny, soft hand. Even if I knew that I wouldn't make anything better, it was maybe also worth getting into contact with her again since we didn't have many chances in the past few weeks. The court had brought us close together again, but as of yesterday, I knew that my abstinence had just made everything better in between us rather than worse. Lust and desire had been in the air as I finally had the chance to stop my primary celibate life for a few minutes. To be in her was like heaven, and I had never imagined it to be such a beautiful place to be since I wasn't religious in any way. Our interaction wasn't the most innocent thing to do. However, I didn't care. I had never cared. I may have changed and been more concerned with everything I was doing in public, but behind the scenes, I could still be the man I wanted to be and was. Finally, I understood that my brothers were obsessed with being emotionless but still satisfied, since he always had the chance to be who he was with and whom he trusted—Lusie and me.

"We're continuing with the accusations against the pharmaceutical industry, "Fav. Pharmaceutics," and ending the court against its leader, Doctor Nathaniel Favouner himself, for now, since we have the facts that we need to make the final court and decision by tomorrow," they explained, and I tensed, wondering if everything that had been said was enough to make a fitting punishment for him. I was wondering if there was any fitting punishment for such a person. Setting him in prison was one thing, but what about the poor souls who had to suffer their entire lives from the past events? In our world, the word "justice" just existed as a matter of what we thought would be the best to do for a primary time range. That there wasn't any kind of chance to balance the count of people's lives that they had lost because of him, nor those that may still be alive but didn't have any chance to come away from the trauma and live a normal life with the past events, made it a compromise rather than a fair complaint between the two parts.

"The first accusation we are going to hear now is the medicaments themselves. To this connected are the high drug prices, their safety concerns, and the lack of transparency," the president announced while everybody prepared themselves with what they wanted to say. While I just sat there doing nothing but holding Lusie's hand, having nothing to say or no chance to be able to help in any other way than what I already had done at their doctor's enlightening and researching houses.

"We start with the complaints and facts you have found," he gave the word to our side, and Nathen's lawyer stood up at once to prepare everything, also with the video material, which I had made, while having his notes for that on the other hand, prepared with his speech as a good lawyer, which he definitely was, at least compared to the other one we were speaking against. He may have had a harder job by trying to prove the public wrong with no facts at all. However, the way he had been speaking and the arguments he had been making were not of any quality at all.

"While the high drug prices are more of a fact than anything I want to argue for, it would be easier to show why they are too high connected to the information of how they calculate them. If we take a look at their safety concern, it is with the medicamentation that they create exactly..." Before he could finish the sentence, the lawyer or the pharmacist cut him angrily off.

"Objection, this is top secret information, which might be used wrongly by other pharmaceutical industries by giving them any attention here." He tried to stop him from revealing the hard facts of their uncertainties, which led to a few seconds of silence. The judges whispered something to each other while the rest of the room was in complete silence.

"We'll skip the pictures of their labours here in the court; send me them too with the explanation that you would have given here," the judge figured out, which didn't please the public, which of course also wanted to see how their drugs there created. Unrest, no satisfaction, and some even dared to scream their unpleasantness throughout the room, which wouldn't last long since they would inform them that they would be banned out if they didn't get themselves together.

Silence, but still the knowledge that nobody liked the judge's acceptance of the complaint there loudly, for nobody to oversee.

"In that case, I would like to get further into the doctor's enlightening's that they have made and the lack of information and tests that they really had about the medication that they recommended and paid them to prescribe." The lawyer didn't see any hint of that; he was taken in surprise or was out of his theme, which he wanted to say. Easily, he took the photos I had made away to get the video from the enlightenment instead, while he continued to talk about the accusations we made about what they had been doing, saying and lying to not only the doctor in the video but also to the public, which had to take their medications.

In the video, you could see the doctors who listened to the untrue facts that were named. I also filmed the papers, which should have had what they were saying written on them, but as we had to improvise and there were no facts at all, these parts were empty, just with the structure of what it was and a few details about how it should help the patient "cure.".

Later, I had also filmed that each doctor would get other prizes for selling the medicament, which included the large range of salary they would get from it and how much the industry really made with that. In it, the pharmacist himself spoke out directly that the regular customers would get more for selling the money, even if altogether it wasn't even 20% of the money they made with each medication per patient.

With each second that passed and every further word that was being said, I saw them turn white and red in frustration, anger, and the inability to do anything against the facts I had caught. Of course, they could call them out as untrue too, but they aren't able to do anything against what has been said there before on the videos, which we had to prove.

"Does the accused have any explanation for how such videos could be tokenized?" The judge changed the point of view of the court to theirs, while the pharmacist just looked at his lawyer, not wanting to say anything himself.

"The accusation at exactly this medicamentation might be true, which doesn't include any others despite this, since it had some problematics with the production and creation," the lawyer agreed, excluding that any other drugs had been lied over at such enlightening's, which luckily was a fact we too could prove wrong. Finally, they had come in catch-22 with their lies. I smiled, satisfied at the facts, as Nathen's lawyer started again.

"Objection, we have other filming that proves this statement wrong," he called out, and after they had seen the second, it was more obvious than ever before how uncomfortable the pharmacist's side was with not having anything to prove that wrong anymore.

"Was that too a medicine that had problematics before the Enlightenment but still was given out to the public as tested and qualified?" the judge asked them calmly, and they both looked at each other before the pharmacist took the word by himself.

"We're judged for not publishing how we're making our medicines and form where everything comes; by a clinic there, you would **not** have known what you are getting at all? Do I understand that, right?" He judged us for the fact that we didn't publish our "medication," which we chose not to do since it was so simple that surely nobody would have believed us anyway.

"If you want to have a court against them, I would rather like you to make a new one, since you aren't going to come far by doing this here right now," the judge said without any sense of threat or humour, with the expression he had the entire time: Camly, neutral, dangerous.

"It might be better to continue with your witness, which might have further details," the judge pointed out, and Greg, one of the pharmacist's closest researchers, stepped a little unhelpful to the front of the room, where a microphone would make his unsure voice even louder.

"I know both my workplace, colleagues, and medications very well. My workplace is tiny, but clean and sterile. Always. My colleagues are intelligent, really good researchers who desperately try to do their best each day." Until now, he hadn't lied. Everything that had been said was a matter of point of view, despite the area in which their job was based. There, it really was always clean. It was almost too clean. You got to wonder if they worked there at all when you stepped into the house.

"About the medication," he didn't find the right words, and silence appeared as everybody waited for him to continue. Surely almost everybody in the public has had some of the drugs before; they may even have had bad experiences with them already. In these words, he had to choose wisely. Very wisely.

"The ingredients are from the same places, which our industry thinks of as trustworthy," he said. He didn't look anywhere but wide-eyed at the table in front of him. I am obviously struggling with finding the right words and not saying anything wrong.

"The prizes are for partly years of research for finding the right solutions to help you, the public, get healthy again," he smiled while he looked at the publicum for a while, but as their response was nothing but cold stares, he gave his attention to the microphone unsurely again.

"For the complications, I am sorry, but keep in mind that we are all humans too. Mistakes happen. Even if they should not, it is hard to get along without making any." He tried to be logical, but with a second thought, this was the agreement that they hadn't tested anything before they released it. If they had done that, almost nobody would have gotten damaged at all.

"Thank you, Mr. Hardstyle, but I have one last question: if you are that convinced with the methods of your pharmaceutical industry," the judge said while he didn't look at him but in some of his notes, which lay in front of him, searching for the proof for the question he had in mind.

"Would you tell me why your wife, who had a cancer diagnosis, wasn't treated in a hospital with, for example, radiation therapy or medicamentation, like every one of your other patients?" He asked him while he leaned forward to become even more present, almost like a threat of not saying the truth. I saw Greg swallowing deeply, looking to the side of him, to his chef. He couldn't help him anymore, either. The truth wouldn't help him, since I could imagine what she had been doing at our clinic.

"It was complicated," he said after a while of death-like silence, while he tried to figure out what would harm both him and the industry as little as possible.

"It wasn't my idea. I wanted to treat her normally, even going with her to a public hospital," as once he had started, the truth flooded out of him as nothing. Loyalty to a cheater was always the best. You should have seen the pharmacist's expression as the worker he trusted most stabbed the knife in his back.

Chapter 13

At first, everyone had been staring at me like I was the worst human they had ever seen in their poor lives. Now, they did that in another way. It was more like I wasn't a human at all. Excluded from their race. It's not worth belonging to anything anymore. Less worth to them than shit. Then there is their daily garbage. Less worth than everything they could imagine. What did this do to me? Nothing. I knew that I had done everything right. Always. They gave me the salary I wanted and what I deserved.

As Hardstyle stood up, he looked at me for a hint of a second and whispered "sorry" to me. Wasted energy. How could somebody be that stupid and tell everybody that the rest of our researchers are as intelligent as him? I think even the worst had a higher IQ than that **former** employee.

"Do you have any complaints with the statements of Greg Hardstyle?" The judge asked us the worst question he could have in mind. What was I about to say? That he didn't have any props? Or rather, that everything was right and that I am proud of what I've done?

"There was never any attention to the fact that their statistics were better than ours. That was a **private** clinic, which did have the opportunity to choose who they thought would have a chance to heal." The lawyer cut me off once I had finished my sentence, but I still wanted to continue.

"Objection: the clinic never chose their patients based on ethnicity, look, age, race, origin, or any other personal details that could have influenced the life-risk after the cancer diagnosis." I took a deep breath while the judge accepted their objection. It wasn't like I had judged them for it; I just wanted to get any kind of point that wouldn't let me fall further floors down on the ground while they threw me out of the fucking window.

"However, what I wanted to make clear about the sake of Mr. Greg Hardstyle is very much that we needed anybody who took care of getting facts out of how our opponent worked." Maybe they got to a game to cut me off, but again, they didn't let me finish my speech.

"Opponent? Doctor Favouner, is that how you have seen the tiny clinic?" The judge judged me again for every word I had been saying. Weren't they supposed to be neutral until they gave me the punishment, they thought I deserved?

"I didn't think about him as such, even if he competed with me and took away the wealthier patients from us. What I was referring to be the primary stadium we are in here at the court," I pointed out, and even if I tried to sound calmly, I heard in my own voice that I'd gotten a little pissed at them already now—long before we were finished.

"It was the only possibly we had, or I had, which made me behold Mr. Hardstyle at work while his wife got treated for her diagnosis," I explained, and he frowned at me, surely not understanding why that was the case. Therefore, I continued without any questioning for that.

"Since it is not long away and even closer to his primary home," I explained, and he noted everything down without any further statements. Luckily. I hated to talk in front of people who didn't appreciate me or dwell on my work. They didn't see all the work I had put inside it, nor did they see what a responsibility I had every single day of my fucking life.

"If there aren't any further arguments to the medicamentation use, prizes, and origin, it would surely be time to continue with the next complaints," the judge looked to each of us, and as nobody said anything, he started to tell the next themes.

"The next judges are for intellectual property rights, overprescribing, overuse, and health inequality, which are partly strongly connected to the last ones but still have to get their own arguments," he explained while he leaned back into his chair, waiting for my **opponents** to start.

"The high cost of patented medications can limit access to essential treatments, particularly in regions where generic alternatives may be unavailable due to patent protection. While the use of trademarks to promote brand-name medications over generic alternatives developed by Fav. Pharmaceutics can contribute to higher drug prices and limit patient choice, particularly in markets with limited competition," their lawyer explained firmly every detail of the "dilemma" of not only our but each single pharmaceutical industry. Something that provoked me, since it sounded like it was only mine, had been in this conversation.

"Their trade secrets to conceal potential safety risks or adverse effects of medications developed by Fav. Pharmaceutics can undermine public health and safety by limiting access to critical information for healthcare providers and patients. Additionally, design protections may also be used to prolong market exclusivity for minor modifications or variations of existing medications developed by Fav. Pharmaceutics, delaying the availability of generic alternatives and contributing to higher drug prices." He finished his speech, which was connected to intellectual property rights, but wouldn't give me more than a second to relax before he already continued with the others.

"Also, the prioritisation of profits over patient welfare by encouraging healthcare providers to prescribe their medications excessively. Increased prescription rates result in higher sales volumes and revenue for the company, driving financial growth and shareholder returns. Which they get out of their aggressive marketing tactics, such as direct-to-consumer advertising, physician incentives, or the named doctor enlightenment, to promote their medications and expand their market share. By influencing prescribing habits and fostering a culture of overprescribing, the company can increase demand for its products and maintain a competitive edge in the pharmaceutical market" I was almost rolling my eyes already. What did they want from us? That we worked for free?

"They exert undue influence on healthcare providers through educational programmes, sponsored events, and financial incentives, encouraging them to prescribe medications unnecessarily or inappropriately. This influence creates a conflict of interest and compromises the integrity of medical decision-making, leading to overprescribing and potential harm to patients. Since it has aggressive sales targets and quotas for its sales representatives, it incentivizes them to promote medications aggressively and maximise prescription volumes. Pressure to meet sales goals can lead to overpromoting medications, regardless of patient need or clinical appropriateness, contributing to overprescribing and potential adverse outcomes". He didn't get distracted by anything; he was fully concentrated on naming the facts he had figured out and getting them out in a way that was understandable for everyone who was here. Not using complicated words or hiding behind anything, he just would say it, even if he hadn't found real proofs for it. For each statement, he would take one on the large screen so that everybody could see it.

"In some cases, as we already have heard, they exploit loopholes in regulatory frameworks or lax oversight mechanisms to engage in overprescribing practices. Limited enforcement of prescribing guidelines or inadequate monitoring of pharmaceutical marketing activities can enable the company to pursue profit-driven strategies at the expense of patient safety and public health. All the named statements lead us to health inequality," he continued, while I was almost astonished over how much my "son" was willing to pay for getting me in jail. This advocate surely wasn't the cheapest he could have found, but for his job, he really did well. Much better than mine, at least.

"Imagine that they implement differential pricing strategies, charging higher prices for medications in regions with greater purchasing power while offering discounts or lower prices in low-income areas. This can exacerbate health inequality by making essential medications inaccessible to disadvantaged populations who cannot afford them at market prices." Now he showed a cart with the sources standing underneath, where we had sold one drug for which there was a there was a difference in price in different areas. I wondered if his sources were even illegal. As long as I knew, we never published anything alike or at all related to our practice.

"Which leads us to the fact that the Fav. pharmaceuticals may prioritise the marketing and distribution of profitable medications over essential but less lucrative drugs, resulting in shortages or limited availability of critical treatments for certain diseases or conditions. This disproportionately affects underserved communities with limited access to healthcare resources, exacerbating health disparities and compromising patient outcomes. Which might be a reason for their want of getting the "PVT clinic cancrocum" away?" he explained. It was so logical that I had to remind myself that it was against me before I almost started to believe it myself.

"The last thing I want to say before I give my word away again is about the prioritised research and development initiatives that cater to profitable markets or prevalent diseases prevalent in affluent populations, neglecting the healthcare needs of marginalised or neglected communities. This selective focus on profitable ventures may lead to a lack of investment in treatments for rare diseases, neglected tropical diseases, or conditions prevalent in low-income regions, perpetuating health inequality and neglecting the health needs of vulnerable populations." His pathetic explanations made it harder for me to catch the public's hearts, but I had already given up on them. What I cared for was the judge's head, which couldn't set anyone of us in prison for what he had been saying. It may influence the feelings, but there wasn't any law that went against us for doing what we had to do to earn enough money, and maybe a little more.

"Thank you, Mr. Morgan. Now the word to the accused for all that." The judge gave me his attention again, and before my lawyer began to stammer anything again, I took the word by myself.

"Impressive sources, which I would like to check the legality of later. However, before you stop," I made a move with my hand, which made him close his mouth again since he had already been on his way of objecting to what I wanted to say and cutting me off, which made me even angrier.

"I want to make something clear again, something that I hope everybody knows already. It is not only ours but every single pharmaceutical industry that has the conflict of having to make money from others sicknesses. For making it clear again. With the money I get from the medications, I have to pay over a hundred employees, who desperately try to help our society by creating new drugs every single day. Not only researching, but also marketing and production are parts of our jobs." I spoke slowly to point these out clearly to everybody. For a while, the room was silent with not a single act, but then the lawyer from him would reach up his hand to try to get to speak again. Already then, I wanted to go out and get home, accepting whatever punishment I would get for that. Wasn't it possible to behold the word for more than a minute? Did they have to talk 80% of the time? It was me who had to try to explain everything in a minute. If that wasn't hard enough, surely impossible, then I didn't know what it was.

"By your explanation, I would like to remind you that the testing should be an even larger part than the researching, since you didn't name it at all." He pointed out my mistake, and my head turned surely almost as red as fire. Why did they bother to point out our testing every single time? There was nothing to say about it. We did it often. Sometimes we didn't know the time before our release date, but we tried at least to test it in any way before we sold it. There wasn't anything further to do about this, was there?

Chapter 14

It was already getting a little late. Much later than it had gotten yesterday. Tomorrow, at the same time, we would be home and know how everything had ended. I was really looking forward to that. An end. A new start to another part of our lives. Deen would overtake the role as a businessman, while Nathaniel's future would be decided tomorrow.

Deen had been holding my hand for most of the time. It comforted me, yes, but still, I wondered if he did it a lot for being calmer himself. Even if he had pretended to listen the entire time, I could see his eyes sometimes looking at anything else while his mind made a journey. Surely to his own clinic, which he had to let go of for a few days now. Three altogether, but still he didn't seem pleased by letting it go without him for further hours, so days were not what he had wanted at all. However, for his brother, he may even tear it down. Even if Deen wasn't anybody who pretended to care a lot about anything other than himself, I was sure to know it better than the façade he had built up to be otherwise than Nathaniel. Well, he was, but not in a bad way. Just completely otherwise. Inconvincible. Indescribable. Unchangeable.

"The last hearing today is about political influence, which I would like the complaining to start with." The judge hadn't the same kind of energy in his voice anymore than at the start of the day.

Understandable, since he had to listen and note everything while figuring out the best way to judge the pharmacist and his company for what they had done.

"Thank you. If we start with why they would do that, of course since they want to shape regulatory policies and decisions in their favour, leading to a phenomenon known as regulatory capture. By lobbying government officials and regulatory agencies, Fav. Pharmaceutics can influence the drafting of laws and regulations governing the pharmaceutical industry, potentially weakening oversight and accountability mechanisms. This can result in lax enforcement of safety standards, expedited approval processes for new drugs, and limited competition from generic alternatives, ultimately compromising public health and safety." Each time he spoke, I was impressed by how easily he tried to explain such hard facts.

My thought was that this would be done similarly to win the attention and appreciation of the public. Even if it wouldn't help us against the judge in the end, I could imagine that Nathaniel had told his lawyer of his future plans for a new clinic. If he wanted to start anything alike, it would be best to have the public on his side to get as many new patients as possible. Since he wasn't hard to like, I decided that this would be a problem anyway. The only fact that scared people was surely his extreme lack of privacy. However, after this, that could change; his name, ancestry, and reason for being against them would be known everywhere and understood. That I was sure of.

"Fav. Pharmaceutics' political influence extended to healthcare policy decisions, particularly those related to drug pricing and access. By lobbying policymakers and lawmakers, Fav. Pharmaceutics can resist efforts to implement price controls or negotiate lower drug prices, thereby maintaining high profit margins at the expense of affordability and accessibility for patients. This can result in exorbitant costs for essential medications, forcing individuals to forgo treatment or bear financial burdens that strain healthcare systems and exacerbate health inequalities." The pharmacist himself had his head in his hand. Like they were the only protection he still had. With each argument, it seemed like the large man turned into a tiny mouse, which hopefully wouldn't sneak away from us before he had solved the punishment he deserved.

"Fav. Pharmaceutics searched to block or undermine legislative initiatives aimed at promoting transparency, accountability, and reform within the pharmaceutical industry. By opposing measures such as drug pricing transparency laws, patent reform initiatives, or efforts to increase access to generic medications, Fav. Pharmaceutics can protect its market dominance and profit margins at the expense of public interest. This can perpetuate a lack of transparency in drug pricing, hinder competition, and impede efforts to address affordability and accessibility issues." While he explained the facts, he always pointed out where he had gotten them from and what the texts or pictures were on the large screen. The judges wrote faster than I could think, trying hard to put everything down on paper, even if they surely would get it afterwards anyway.

"The last statement I want to make for the rest of the day," he started, and I had contrasting feelings about the fact that he would be over soon. On one side, I was exhausted and almost ready to go to bed before eating anything or doing anything else. On the other hand, I wondered if everything that had been said was enough for us to win the case. Additionally, I somehow liked to hear him talking. It wasn't boring at all. Especially to see the way he had worked interested me a lot. How somebody could find such information, even if he had a long time, was still impressive. Even the pharmacist wondered where he had gotten it from and if it was legal at all. However, since the sources stood under each other, I was sure that he had been doing his job right and found the information anywhere it was allowed.

"Their political influence extended to research funding and educational initiatives in the healthcare sector. By providing financial support to academic institutions, research organisations, and healthcare professionals, Fav. Pharmaceutics shapes research agendas, influences treatment guidelines, and promotes favourable perceptions of its products. This leads to conflicts of interest, biassed research outcomes, and overprescribing of brand-name medications, potentially compromising patient care and public health outcomes. Again, we can connect the facts to each other. Still, they are showing us singular criminal acts that they **have** done." without any thanking for the attention, just with a simple nod to show everybody that he was finished, he went back to his place and sat down. I didn't hear what they said, but I saw that Nathaniel talked or whispered something to him.
"Good, then I would like the Fav. pharmaceuticals to end the second day of court with whatever they have to say against the named

facts," the judge said calmly while he leaned back. Knowing that they were not as well prepared and wouldn't let him write two novels in the course of the hours that we had been here today.

"I appreciate the hope you all lay in me still, even if the named facts look that realistically," the pharmacist said ironically, again not letting his lawyer talk. At first, it was him who had refused to say anything, but somehow he might have figured out that the unsureness of his representation wasn't any good for them at all, even if I wondered if there was anything better to say for their innocentness. There was no fact that they could show to them all since they thought about it as already too much of what we had been saying. Everything was considered a top secret. Why, surely everybody could imagine.

"My industry, Fav. Pharmaceutics, is engaged in political influence to advocate for policies that support innovation, research, and patient access to life-saving medications. By working with policymakers and regulatory agencies, Fav. Pharmaceutics can help shape healthcare policies that promote investment in research and development, streamline regulatory processes for drug approval, and ensure fair pricing practices. This is a new collaboration that will hopefully lead to the development of breakthrough treatments, increased access to medications for patients in need, and advancements in public health outcomes by taking donations from them instead of such high prices" He cleared his throat before he continued shortly afterwards.

"Additionally, Fav. Pharmaceutics' involvement in political influence can foster partnerships with government agencies and healthcare stakeholders to address pressing health challenges, such as pandemics or rare diseases, as we had with Corona, through collaborative efforts and resource mobilization. Overall, our engagement in political influence can contribute to a more vibrant and responsive healthcare ecosystem that benefits patients, healthcare providers, and society as a whole." It was maybe the best the pharmacist had said the entire time. It was not good for us, as it was at the end of the day, and we wouldn't have any further time to try to tear their argumentation down again. However, the judge had our facts. What he had been saying was logical and emphatic, but still without any proofs or sources.

"Do you want to say anything against that?" The judge asked us, and while I didn't see their expression, I heard an unimpressed chuckle before his lawyer started to speak.

"If it is that new, I wonder where the money has gone and why, after my research, it has already been a strong political influence for more than five years. Additionally, the prizes haven't gone in that direction since then. No. The other one. However, I don't want to start another discussion and let the statements stand as they lay here in the air for you to consider until tomorrow." He never spoke pleasantly to them. He used them more as a tool than anything else, which might help him get his client anywhere further towards his goal. He had a strong personality, but that was right here, I wondered. Even if all his speeches had been very good, it might still not be enough. Maybe it was never enough. This, we would get to know tomorrow. on the final day of the judge.

Chapter 15

The next day, I woke up with a feeling of uncertainty. Soon, it would disappear. That I had been asleep for a few hours showed me already that I saw a positive possibility of getting what I wanted out of the case. In two hours, the final judge of appeals will start. Even if everybody was still asleep, I figured it would be best to stand up and get something to eat before we got to the last day of the court together.

With some rolls in one hand and some cold cuts in the other, I came back again. Both of them were already awake, and well, they may hadn't imagined that I would come back that soon.

"Good morning to you too," I said as nobody recognised me. They had been focused on each other. Lusie remained calm, but Deen jumped out of the bed like a frightened cat. I looked at him amused and a little not understanding; what did he think that I would do to him if he had some fun with Lusie? It was the best that could happen—not anything I wouldn't support as long as it was consensual.

"Where are you?" he asked while he tried to take some clothes unhelpful on himself. I had seen him undressed surely a thousand times before; additionally, not only him but many other men, since I had been working at a public hospital too. However, in that moment, he thought about everything, including distraction, rather than relaxation.

"Get us some breakfast; we will have to go to court soon," I explained, and I wondered if he had forgotten, pushed the thought away, or knew it exactly and was just a little ashamed of everything, so that he needed to say anything. May the last one be the most likely statement.

We ate some breakfast together in silence. Someday I would talk to him about how it wasn't any problem for me if they did whatever they wanted to do like that, but at first I wanted to finish everything before I said anything, which I would regret later. Even if I was sure that I wouldn't, it was never smart to say more than necessary or anything you haven't thought 100% about; it wasn't considered very well.

As we apparently didn't have anything to say to each other now, we would also go in silence to the courthouse. Before we stepped in, Lusie gave me a soft kiss on the cheek.
"Everything will be fine; if not, we'll make it even better than you can imagine, okay?" She was sometimes so sweet that she was caring about what I was thinking about. Most often, she was even right; even this here was an easy guess. I smiled lightly and nodded towards her in support, even if it was less important if I was fine, more so if she was.

The judge appeared precisely, but all of them looked exhausted before the court had started. They had some hours to figure everything out. Some days to inform themselves about everything they needed. Still, it wasn't easy to decide about not only one, but maybe thousands of lives in their country. The job they had, I didn't want to have at all. Even if I could decide a lot as a doctor, my only task was to save humans a good quality of life.

"Yesterday, we've considered valid punishments for both cases," the judge said, starting the day without an "Hello" or "Good morning" as always. He didn't want to waste his time or ours, and I think we all appreciated it. Especially today, everybody just wanted to hear the final end of everything.

"If we start with the singular case against Doctor Nathaniel Favouner," he said, looking into his notes rather than at him in person. Understandable, since I couldn't tell if I would be able to do so in his position either.

"If we start with the discrimination against women, Dr. Favouner's discrimination against women under his care and within his pharmaceutical company is an abuse of power and authority. Alongside fines and mandatory sensitivity training for himself and his employees, he must publicly acknowledge his wrongdoing and actively promote gender equality initiatives. Fav. Pharmaceutics should be required to implement diversity and inclusion programmes, and Dr. Favouner should personally fund initiatives supporting women's rights" parts of the publicum laughed and cheered shortly, while it still wasn't the punishment I had waited for. It wasn't even his; I had it in mind while finding an appreciable end to the court.

"Secondly, the harming of others both physically and psychologically; he should face a significant prison sentence and financial restitution to his victims. Fav. Pharmaceutics should also be held accountable for any negligence contributing to these harms, with mandatory safety and ethical compliance audits imposed on the company upon Dr. Favouner's release." It was better, more connected to the industry, but there wasn't a final judge until now.

"For the child abuse Dr. Nathaniel Favouner's betrayal of trust as both a medical professional and a pharmaceutical industry owner in perpetrating child abuse is deeply reprehensible. In addition to a substantial prison sentence, his medical license should be permanently revoked, and Fav. Pharmaceutics should face hefty fines for its association with such misconduct. Dr. Favouner must also undergo extensive rehabilitation and counselling, with a strict ban on any future involvement with children or pharmaceutical products." I felt that I was more satisfied with him being set in prison than free. Still, it wasn't a solution to just put criminal people into a boiler. Maybe a primary isolation, but it wouldn't help them become better humans at all.

"For the spying and blackmailing of the PVT clinic, Dr. Favouner's abuse of his professional position for personal gain through spying and blackmailing warrants severe legal consequences. In addition to imprisonment and fines, Fav. Pharmaceutics should be subject to heightened scrutiny and oversight, with mandatory transparency measures implemented to prevent further abuses of power." Even if he had put on a mask to hide his feelings about it, I could see his body tense and his frown while he went deeper and deeper, longer and longer into a life-long prison sentence.

"The last punishment against him in person is the bombing of the clinic, which causes many deaths." For a moment, everything was silent. I could hear the harsh breathing of the relatives, since this wasn't anything for me but mainly for them. I was hoping that he would get his well-deserved punishment.

"Dr. Favouner's involvement in such a violent act resulting in the loss of life demands the strictest punishment available under the law. He should receive a life sentence without parole, and Fav. Pharmaceutics should be dissolved, with its assets liquidated to compensate the victims' families and support community initiatives against violence. Rehabilitation efforts for Dr. Favouner may be pursued, but justice for the victims and their families must remain the primary focus." Some cheered, others cried. It was what they had been waiting for. The first step was finished. The only one who had lost until now was the person who deserved to lose everything.

"Let us continue with the Fav. pharmaceuticals at once," the judge said loudly through the microphone, even if his voice surely would have been hearable without it too.

"For the high drug prices, Fav Pharmaceutics must pay significant fines proportional to the extent of price gouging observed in their pharmaceutical products. These fines should be calculated based on the difference between the production cost and the retail price, with penalties increasing for essential medications and those with minimal alternatives" acceptance, no applaud or anything. Silence covered the room, letting him continue to say his punishments.

"Related to the drug safety concerns, the company should be subjected to hefty fines for any documented instances of negligence in ensuring the safety and efficacy of their drugs. The fines should be calibrated based on the severity of the safety concerns and the potential harm caused to consumers. Additionally, they will have to pay every single person who has been harmed in any way by taking untested medication," his words stayed in the room. We are all there, not just me, waiting for anything further. What? I couldn't say. I didn't know it either. Justice had never been easy, and it would always remain hard like it was.

"The lack of transparency should be solved and punished, and the favourite pharmaceuticals must be penalised for their lack of transparency in pricing, research, and development expenditures. Fines should be imposed for failure to disclose relevant information to regulatory authorities and consumers, with escalating penalties for repeated offences." It was better than nothing, still not satisfying me fully.

"The Fav Pharmaceutics has engaged in intellectual property rights abuses, such as patent manipulation or infringement, and they should be required to pay substantial fines as restitution to affected parties. Additionally, they may be subjected to legal actions by affected individuals or competing pharmaceutical companies." It was justice. What they could do. Maybe there wasn't even a chance to do anything further. Still, they couldn't punish them in the way they deserved, since they were important to the state too. In the end, the only reason I came all the way to the Supreme Court.

"The next is about overprescribing and overuse. Here, fines should be imposed on Fav Pharmaceutics for any evidence of promoting overprescribing or overuse of their medications through aggressive marketing tactics or misleading advertising. These fines should serve as a deterrent against unethical marketing practices and the exploitation of vulnerable patient populations." I looked towards my lawyer, who nodded as the only one satisfied by each statement. He really had done a good job. Additionally, he was surely already aware of what they would say, since he had been a judge himself for many years and knew exactly the possibilities of such a punishment" act for an entire industry.

"Favourite pharmacies should be required to contribute a significant portion of their profits towards initiatives aimed at reducing health inequality, such as subsidising medications for low-income populations, funding community health programmes, or supporting research into neglected diseases. Failure to comply should result in substantial financial penalties." The last statement was coming soon. Until he was finished with that, I had to figure out if I could be satisfied with it. It was what it was, and alike, it would be practiced. Still, something inside me told me that years of suffering deserved a harsher punishment, while the other side knew that nothing further was possible in a legal way.

"The last punishment for the day against Fav Pharmaceutics is that because they have been engaged in undue political influence through lobbying or campaign contributions, they should be fined for attempting to subvert democratic processes and undermine public health policies. These fines should be commensurate with the extent of their influence and the potential harm caused to public interests." After his words had been echoing throughout the room, he stood up, like everybody else, and everybody left the room, and I realised—that was it.

Lifelong prison sentence, rehabilitation, and making the former pharmacist aware of his actions against women, children, and all those who were damaged by him. While his former industry had to start many courses on ethical issues and would surely be supervised, at least for the next few years, they had to pay large sums to everybody who had been harmed by their earlier mistakes and to themselves.

"Satisfied?" My lawyer nudged me carefully while he looked at me, waiting for an answer.

"Somehow, I may think yes," the words echoed through me, and a relieved feeling was placed in me, which I had never felt before. In some way, it even felt good. Very good.

"You may always have the chance,
but whoever reacts faster runs
away further."

Part 2

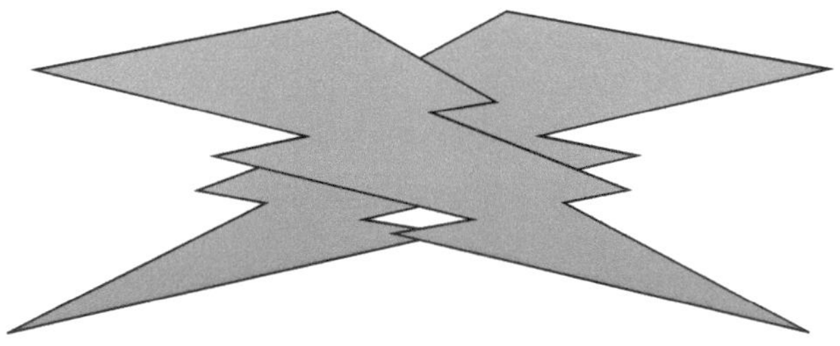

Chapter 1

Change could be everything. You could get a new job and become a completely different person. An accident could happen to somebody you have loved for years. It doesn't have to be such a strong and formative experience. It could also be just to stand up and know exactly what you want to do. Planning, which I earlier hated, became one of my strongest and most important friends to start the clinic in a doable way. Without any notes in mind, my day would have to last at least twice as long. No free time or breaks would exist.

"Thank you, Miss Stowell." She'd been taking part in my job the last day. Even if you didn't need a doctor for the withdrawal itself, it wasn't unusual that anybody hurts themselves by going through the hardest time of their lives. I had experienced it myself, and it has been unbearable. Worse than I'd ever expected. I hadn't only experienced it once, and not twice either, but each time it got worse. Maybe because I didn't get younger either. However, my body didn't appreciate the substances I had, and I learned to give my body what it wanted. We had to remain friends for many years, so it wasn't smart to start fights with him now.

"No problem at all, Mr. Miller. If you have anything further, I will always be there to help you with everything," she offered kindly, and before I could say anything further, somebody appeared behind me. His intense gaze I felt already burning in my back. Living and knowing him for years would never change this kind of response in my body to his presence. Even if we had seen us yesterday after the court too, it wasn't more than the drive back. They had let me out of the clinic at once so that I could start to do everything I had missed. Sleeping was important. To me, it was sometimes even necessary for a normal life. However, three days of abstinence shaped the clinic at once. Not for the patients, but for example, on the stack of paperwork, you could see the need for me easily.

Additionally, I would make a health check for each patient. As my dear brother appeared behind me, much sooner than I had expected them, I was done with around 40% of them.
"Good morning. I didn't know that you would want to eat breakfast here too." I looked at him while I noticed Lusie was behind him. She didn't look at me, but throughout the clinic, she was trying to figure out the primary situation.

"Thanks for the offer, but I think we wanted to help you, but you can join us this evening instead." He looked behind him to Lusie, who turned her attention to us again at once. Her white, brown eyes faced me like the eyes of an angel. Shimmering in the light of the clinic She smiled politely, but it didn't look like that. Not for me. Maybe for everybody else in the room, and maybe it was even the purpose. How could I know? She was extremely good at hiding her feelings, something I didn't appreciate at all. I was already so bothered by my brother, but it wasn't much easier to see her smile and not know if she was sad, angry, frustrated, or just happy.

"Hi." She created me and didn't stop to smile. Whatever the intention of this was, it affected me so much that I almost automatically smiled towards her too. Otherwise, my brother, I still didn't care about showing my emotions in public.

"Hi to yourself, darling." I winked at her, but for a hint of a second, her smile widened and then faded as she looked behind my back. I frowned in disappointment, but as I turned around to see what had tokened her out of nowhere and made me lose my eye contact with her, I saw just the nurse I had been talking to. Nobody else was there. There was no reason for her to react alike; it was almost out of shock, while she hadn't controlled her feelings for the hint of a second.

"You show us we could help you with, or do you, brother, stand here and talk for the rest of the day?" Nathaniel bothered me and took my thoughts away. Of course, that was the reason that they were here, but still, I wanted to see and know what had happened behind me. It was seldom that Lusie showed her real feelings, and if she did, it was because of something unexpected that happened. Anything that made her lose control for a hint of a second about her emotion control.

"It depends on what you want to do. I do have more than enough." I turned around, and they followed me without a second word.

Lusie had sorted out all the paperwork, while Nathaniel had done it. It went much faster than expected, and before I could start to worry again about how I would do everything as fast as possible, we were already finished. Three days of work with three people went much faster than you can imagine. Especially if those are the best relations I have and maybe also the smartest people I know.

"Do you have anything else in mind, or can we start already?" Lusie asked me, as I had finished checking the last patient too.

"I have a lot in mind, but nothing is related to the clinic; even if it could possibly be done here," I winked at her, and she laughed while Nathaniel entered the room too.

"Let's head to our first table-meeting then," he said with a soft smile to the two of us as we laughed and smiled together. Sometimes I wondered if this was something he could get jealous about. Sex didn't matter to him, as I had figured out. I could kiss Lusie in front of him; without that, he would even raise an eyebrow. Everything further, it wasn't him either, but me, which I wasn't comfortable with in front of others.

"Thank you for joining us." Lusie shone like the sun itself as we headed to their car.

"I wouldn't have missed it for the world, since you wanted me to be with you." I didn't only say it, I sweated nothing. It was more, much more than that. It made Lusie happy, and this was everything I needed and wanted too. like Nathaniel had explained to me before.

This wasn't to need a person anymore, like it had been before with her. This was love. Nothing is more complicated than that.

"You will see, it isn't only for me. I am sure there are some pretty ladies whom you can throw yourself at too. You know, I am not a switch like you," she explained as we already sat in the public-safe car. Before, this might have provoked me, as I desperately tried to come away from all this kinky stuff. However, now, after I had already tried some things, I had given up on running and started to **go** back again. Step by step. Despite my full appreciation, lust, and desire, there would still be some lessons I had to learn.

I remembered Jake's words often and knew that I wasn't safe enough as a dominant. I didn't know enough about it at all. As a doctor, my anatomy knowledge was very good, but there were a lot of other themes to consider. Where I would start, I couldn't know until now. Just one thing I was quite certain about: with whom I would want to start it. This was a pretty lady, but not "some" pretty lady. It was the only one I was interested in right now, and I hoped that my feelings wouldn't confuse me with any other ideas for the next few hours either.

Chapter 2

"Excuse me, is there any reservation for Longfield today too?" Nathaniel politely asked the girl at the bar. It took her a second to shut her mouth and start thinking, as she had recognized that it had been a question.

"Yes, or no. They wanted me to tell newcomers that they are meeting at the former culture house today, but don't worry, I think they wanted to start half an hour later, so that everybody could join in." I wondered why they would change the location today all of a sudden. Luckily, the girl knew exactly where to go, and in less than fifteen minutes, we had reached the new location.

"Hello, you're new here, right?" A friendly man greeted us, and I stepped back a little in uncertainty since I didn't know anything about anybody. The other location made me a little scared of what would come. It wasn't a normal, official place anymore. There was no public body that could protect us. However, the two brothers had to be enough security for me.

"Yes, we are, but it would be a delight to join you more often too, since we aren't living long away from here at all." Nathaniels form way of talking made me smile again, as I recognised that he probably didn't like such a change at all. It wasn't my part to blame, since he would do it too. I was safe here, I told myself as I looked at the ocean of people in front of me. Altogether, maybe almost a hundred, I would say. I wondered where they came from and if they were here usually or just joining the special event today.

"I would say it's the best day you can start here. We will have a professional arrangement, which is going to talk about what to take care of before starting the pleasure," he said, reaching out his hand to each of us. It was Mr. Longfield, so Xavier Longfield, who organised the weekly meetings at the café.

"Come on, let's get some good places before the best are taken." He led us inside, and I noticed how stiffened and tensed Deen was beside us. I took therefore his ice-cold hand as warm. For a moment, he smiled, appreciating my touch, but then he concentrated himself on the new people, environment, and housing again.

"It will already start in about ten minutes. I've mainly organised it to get some people together and new members interested," he explained on the way. He was an extrovert, maybe almost 5.9 inches tall, and always had a large smile on his lips. It had been easy to start a conversation with him, and I could tell why he chose to organise everything, since the job mainly was about people, which included talking and texting to get the café, whether at weak or other times, like today.

"You said he was a professional; what exactly does that mean?" I asked and wondered if there was a study to take or if it was about the experience you had over the years.

"Well, he goes from place to place to talk about different principles and structures in a BDSM relationship and does his best to make a session in a safe way. However, I think there are plenty of courses that you can take in addition to the experiences you make at our private meetings," he explained easily, but was not able to look me in the eyes.

"You have the private meetings too?" I asked in mind how Jakes had been back in Germany. From everything I had seen until now, that was, by far, the best.

"Yes, or course, we try to make it one or two times each month to any of our places," he explained with an amused smile, and I saw a kid of fire burning in his eyes, as he surely had in mind what happened at whose "private meetings.".

"Can I ask about your position in the BDSM world?" My words left my mouth before I knew what I had asked. It wasn't usual for me to just do what I wondered about or had in mind. Especially such a question there that private, I wasn't a big fan of just asking that as a by-the-way question.

"Of course, that's nothing unusual to ask about here. I am both an experience sub, but I switched more to the dominant side in the past years," he explained with a smile, and I recognised that Deen had started to give the theme a little attention too. Before that, he had been almost desperate to look everywhere, but at the places there, it was possible that anything could happen soon. There was nothing, not even handholding, between the gusts. Yes, some used the opportunity today to wear scene-related clothing and jewellery, but nothing critical at all.

"Hello, dear BDSM interests, scene members, or newcomers. My name is Master Sattler, and today we're going to talk about BDSM from A to Z, so lean back and enjoy the show." A man in his early forties was on the stage. He was dressed in a black suit and tie, with a green eye that shone through the entire room, in contrast to the other "colours" he wears.

"If we start with what we are famous for, even if it shouldn't only be such a large part in our scene but also for every single Vanilla living on our planet earth, the communication before anything starts. So, what do we talk about? A good start might be to initiate an open and honest dialogue with your partner about your interest in BDSM and your desires for the session. Share what aspects of BDSM appeal to you, whether it's exploring power dynamics, sensory play, bondage, or other activities. Encourage your partner there to express their thoughts, feelings, and boundaries as well. Since they are essential in BDSM play to ensure that both partners feel safe and respected, discuss what activities you're comfortable with and what is off-limits. This might include physical boundaries as well as emotional boundaries, which we all have in some ways. Be sure that you are clear and specific about your boundaries and listen attentively to your partner's boundaries **without any** judgement," he pointed out, and I looked towards Deen for a while. It hadn't been his fault since he wasn't accepting himself with the desire in his mind. Still, it had made me much more uncomfortable and uncertain to accept mine, as he had rejected and tried to destroy everything. Punishing me, or us, at the sudden leave to Dubai didn't make it any better at all.

"Many of us, especially newcomers, may even start with safe words or signals, which are crucial for establishing consent and maintaining safety during BDSM play. These are special words or gestures that either partner can use to communicate discomfort, the need to slow down, or the desire to stop the activity altogether. Agree on a safe word or signal that is easy to remember and understand and reaffirm its use before the session begins." At once, I remembered what Nathaniel had said to me almost a year ago. Even if we never had been in need of it, since we didn't come that long, to have in mind that I always was able to stop everything calmed me a lot."

"As in many parts of our lives, negotiation is also a big part here afterwards. It involves discussing and reaching agreements on the specific activities you'd like to engage in during the session. This might include exploring different BDSM techniques such as bondage, impact play, sensation play, role-playing, or other kinks and fetishes. Some may even make a contract to have everything written down, from what each partner likes to the hard limits. Please make sure to prioritise health and safety considerations during your communication and planning process. Discuss any physical health concerns, allergies, or medical conditions that may impact your play. Consider the use of safe sex practices, such as using condoms or other barrier methods, if applicable. Additionally, make sure you have any necessary equipment or supplies on hand, such as lubricant, first aid supplies, or BDSM gear," he warned, and even if I had never heard of any events that had happened until now, I could tell that it wasn't unlikely that anything happened since it was about physical pleasure you might haven't gotten a part of before.

"If you have all this in mind, I think you are good to go and start the greatest pleasure and make your fantasies and darkest desires come true," he smiled while he continued his speech. He was good at it, even if it surely wasn't anything hard to talk about, since it was, in a way, a kind of hobby or even lifestyle for him.

"In BDSM, consent goes beyond mere acquiescence or the absence of a "no." It requires enthusiastic and active participation from all parties involved. This means that consent should be clearly and enthusiastically communicated, and it should be ongoing throughout the entire session. Partners should express their desires, boundaries, and limits openly and honestly, and they should only engage in activities that all parties have consented to." I remembered how carefully both Jake and Nathaniel had been with me, even if Jake hadn't talked that much compared to him, who always used the best words but unfortunately wouldn't get them to happen.

"In addition to verbal communication, it's important to pay attention to non-verbal cues during a BDSM session. These can include body language, facial expressions, and vocalisations that indicate comfort, arousal, or discomfort. Partners should be attuned to each other's non-verbal cues and be prepared to adjust or stop the play if necessary." Reading minds like Nathaniel or feeling others feelings like Jake was a good characteristic to have, as I realised as he explained it. While I looked for a short moment at Nathaniel, I recognised that not only him but also Deen were very concentrated on each word he said. They didn't even recognise that I had been looking at them. I smiled for a moment before turning my attention back to the speech again. It was amusing that even if Deen never said it, he too was that interested in the same topic. Coincidence or passion—that was the final question.

"Please don't make the same mistake as a good friend of mine and think that the consent is a one-time agreement. It's definitely not. More of an ongoing process that can be revoked at any time. If at any point during the session a partner feels uncomfortable, unsafe, or wants to stop, they have the right to withdraw their consent. It's essential for all parties to respect each other's boundaries and immediately cease any activity if consent is withdrawn. Only then can our scene be safe and get rid of the bad view the vanillas have on us. Yes, we might have some black sheep forever, but they shouldn't define who we really are and what we want to reach with our desires." Once again, my eyes went to search Deen's expression and reaction to what he had been saying. Nothing. An unusual mask was hiding them. Was this already too much for him? Would he ever accept his sexuality as it was and don't pretend like it was anything illegal and incorrect?

Chapter 3

I checked my forehead the second time. There was no note with the word "Vanilla" standing upon it. It seemed like he made a lesson for me to accept and know what everything is about. With each step throughout, I felt more and more personally touched. Each time he said their word for "normal people" again, I twitched and looked towards him at once. Never would he look at me. Always, he seemed as relaxed as before, not as tensed as I was. The worst was that I was the only one who thought about it. Some laughed easily at his jokes; others leaned back with a smile and relaxed completely. Then there was me, arms crossed in front of me, frowning or not looking at the scene at all, legs as tightly squeezed together as possible, to take as little space as possible. Already, it seemed like what I was breathing, touching, and taking wasn't meant for me, but any other person who supported it before now.

"Now you are finished with your session, and here too, we do have an individual ending like with almost everything else. Some might tear apart from each other, especially if you know your partner well. However, since BDSM can be intense and emotionally charged, especially for the submissive partner, Aftercare provides a safe space for participants to process their emotions, decompress, and reconnect with each other on an emotional level. It helps alleviate feelings of vulnerability, anxiety, or guilt that may arise during or after the scene. "Latest now, I checked out for cameras to see if that was a joke. Jake was nowhere to be seen either; it could have been a lesson he had taught me. Never had he listened to me; at once he decided who I was by the simple fact that I didn't want to accept my kinky fantasies. Yes, he was right in a large part, but not all. There are desires I am scared to tell anybody or to let be done. Not only with anybody, but also with me. Both as a switch and with other people, despite Lusie. Nobody was in love with me, but just others. Selfish me might never get enough of having sex with many at once or after one and another. To suppress the thought appeared to be the smartest idea, but that wasn't possible here. Even if he hadn't named my main fantasies, it could have been Deen he said instead of "Vanilla." Jake had written the speech in person, and he was just a doll to present it to us here and now.

"Activities such as bondage, impact play, or sensory deprivation can cause physical sensations like pain, fatigue, or adrenaline rushes. Aftercare involves attending to any physical needs, such as applying ice packs, providing water, or administering first aid if necessary. It helps participants recover and soothes any discomfort or pain." Lusie smiled, like she always did, while a flame burned in her eyes. Nathaniel was relaxed, like he seldom was in public, while he listed each word like it would mean the world to him. I took a deep breath, knowing that if it wouldn't end soon, I had to take a break myself. Of course, we sat in the middle of the room, and it would get hard to come away for just a minute or two. Like this too, it had been decided by anybody who wanted to let me suffer and hear every single word that was said. I listened, and I considered each statement. No propaganda, illogical explanations, or other hints that it was me that he talked too. In the end, it was maybe just me who had made the usual stigmatisations and now thought that everything fitted towards me, perhaps as much as it did to many others too. That is what a good speaker would have done: make every word sound like he was talking to you in person, not in a room filled with hundreds of people. A private lesson in public, just for you, as much for everyone else.

"Since aftercare fosters intimacy and strengthens the bond between partners, it provides an opportunity for cuddling, holding, or gentle touch, which releases oxytocin, the "bonding hormone." This physical closeness reassures both partners of their care and affection for each other, enhancing trust and intimacy in the relationship." that sounded really vanilla-like. Was it what Jake had wanted me to do with his submissiveness, which had dominated me at this time? It didn't sound like him. Neither wanted I nor could I imagine him after a session, caring for anybody in such ways.

"Since our scenes often involve intense role-playing or power dynamics that can blur the lines between fantasy and reality, Aftercare also helps participants transition back to their everyday identities and roles by providing a supportive environment where they can express themselves authentically and feel grounded. "Yes, I had felt rare after the play with her. Somehow, I wondered why there was that much that you had to keep caring about after a lesson. In one way, it was logical; in another, it was over. Ended. No second thought nor ideas; at least that had been sex for me most often. I didn't care about the girl, even if I wouldn't say it. After the interaction, it was clear that everything was done. No more kissing, touching, or sweet words. "Goodbye" or "Where is the shower?" afterwards, never seeing each other again. Ever. And that was good, like it was. I had never missed them. Never had I felt fully satisfied with them, and yes, I know that this isn't fair, but it's like it had been.

"The maybe most known part of why we should have aftercare is the subdrop, which refers to the emotional and physical crash that some submissives may experience after a scene, characterised by feelings of sadness, anxiety, or emotional vulnerability. Topspace, on the other hand, refers to the euphoric state that some dominants may experience during play, followed by a potential comedown. Aftercare helps mitigate the effects of subdrop and topspace by providing comfort, reassurance, and stability." I looked around, just to realise that there still wasn't any camera, nor was Jake himself watching me.

I wouldn't have blamed him, since I really didn't know anything about the scene or its rules while I was playing with his girlfriend. It had been pretty much the same for me and for her too. Not because I was a person who didn't care about other humans and their feelings, no. That wasn't the case at all. I wasn't used to it and didn't know how much she may have suffered afterwards. It had been over; my thoughts were there on other places again, and on these I was. Not taking care of the girl I had just fucked once. Why should I? Now, I wouldn't do the same again. He had made everything clear; as long as the other partner didn't want that either, I wouldn't leave anybody for the next few minutes or hours after normal sex, or maybe even a session. Even if he had talked about BDSM in particular, now I wouldn't be able to give a shit and leave at once after the softest vanilla intercourse either. Thanks for that, whoever is filming or watching this here.

"As we had said before, aftercare provides an opportunity for participants to communicate about the scene, discuss what worked well, and address any concerns or boundaries for future play. It encourages open, honest communication and strengthens the trust and understanding between **both** partners. Don't make the mistake of thinking about the dominant as the strongest, unbreakable one ever. I've been talking to plenty of them who just didn't dare say that they needed it or wanted to have some closeness after the session. Often, these are men who don't show their feelings as usual, and now, after our session, there is no question that they might have any at all, just because they are used to hiding them. Alright?" He asked, and the entire room answered yes at once. It had to have been planned. To say that precisely one word together wasn't possible elsewhere.

"Good, then I think there we are. Now, I have talked a long enough monologue, and you have to be bored to hear a single tone from me. Therefore, I would like to open up for everybody to come on the stage and tell what bothers their thoughts related to our scene or explain further details that they think are important to know for everybody to have in mind. Of course, I will be available afterwards too, if there are some people who aren't comfortable talking through my rotted microphone," he said, and half of the room laughed while nobody stood up. Wasn't this me they were talking to all the time? Hadn't they even placed cameras to watch my reaction to each statement? I dwelled on it now, but still, I felt that addressed, so I stood up and went to the scene myself. To the shock of Lusie and Nathaniel, who may have wondered which thoughts I wanted to share.

"Here we have a brave one," the speaker smiled towards me while some kind of motivating music played in the background. Not like I wouldn't dare turn around anyways by now.

"Who are you? How long have you been in the scene, and which role do you have in it?" not like three, but thousands of questions it appeared for me to be. I took the microphone into my hands while I turned towards him, realising that the light didn't make it possible for me to look into the public without blinding me totally.

"People call me Deen, but nobody of them would have imagined to find me on **this** stage here tonight." I pointed towards the stage while I felt that everything was too late. I had wanted this, so why shouldn't I make it get finished now? In the end, it was too late to turn around by now.

"Not because I would have been too shy to get up here, but maybe because they think that I don't have anything to say about this, to all of you listeners," I pointed with a small smile on my lips towards the public, while the words somehow flooded out of my mouth. I had wanted to say them for a long time. Somehow, it never felt like I would get any kind of answer that I wanted. Here, that was otherwise. There was not only the speaker but also a hundred other kinksters there, and I couldn't imagine that there wasn't at least one of them who knew what to say and mentioned who I was. This was one of the problems I had in this scene; I had to figure out a new me. Even if the idea itself sounded good, practicing it would sound dangerous for somebody with fantasies like mine.

"Why would they believe that? I mean, in your eyes, I can already see it shine as we talk about this. To me, it's obvious that you are interested, as you stand beside me here now." I laughed a little in confusion about his psychoanalysis of me and chose to remain honest, which was the smartest thing I could do. In the end, they might throw me out. This would be good for the part that I never would have to return. On the other side, it didn't seem to me like they weren't open and that anybody would get thrown anywhere, as long as they followed the rules.

"You know what motivated me to come up here?" I asked him, and as he shrugged with a smile on his lips, waiting for my answer like I had suspected, I went on. They got my story—here and now. Nowhere and to no other time else.

Chapter 4

What the hell had happened to Deen? I didn't curse often, nor did I do that to anybody. However, as I saw him there on the stage, in front of everybody, I recognised that there were still parts I didn't know about him. Nathaniel had looked at him sceptically but wasn't as surprised as me; at least he didn't show it at all. Easily, almost like it was his passion, he went up there and started the conversation with the Master Sattler, like everything was planned and they had known each other for a long time. Something bothered me; he had never been that easy or open to anybody of us, but to all whose strangers he was now at once.

"People call me a scene shammer, not because I ever said anything against it, but since I don't accept it. Not for you all, but just for me. I learned to be fine with it if it participated in front of or even beside it. Still, I am fighting with jealousy as anybody touches my girl, but since she isn't mine as a bought object, I had to learn to accept it," he started, and the speaker knew at once what to do with the started conversation in front of everybody.

"Raise your hands if you have felt like Deen before you learned to accept it like it was," he ordered, and I raised my hands, unlikely Nathaniel, but alike at least half of the rest of the publicum. Deen's eyes widened in shock at the fact that so many had felt the same before and didn't find the right words for some seconds.

"Thank you. I appreciate your help and support very much. However, still, it's hard for me to allow myself to think that way and have fantasies," he explained his struggle honestly, and everybody listened to each word he said like they felt it in their hearts.

"If you feel comfortable sharing them with us, we have plenty of time to discuss them or even get others interested in the same on the stage too. Just sit down here; may you relax a little more there and let the kinky word sink into yourself, like a healing potion." They both laughed for a while and said something to each other that I couldn't hear since it wasn't spoken into the microphone.

"Okay, where to start? Well, I consider myself a switch, which means that I have intense fantasies on both sides, which I well struggle with allowing myself to even think about or consider that they might become reality anytime." He said it so easily that it was almost hard to believe that he had mentioned it at all. Like they were there talking about a book they had been reading, not like an everything-changing action, which he definitely had done by getting up on the stage.

"Additionally, I am in love with one person by still having fantasies with others," his words meant for me. That he hadn't trusted me enough to say them while we were there alone anytime before made me flinch for a short second. His eyes searched mine, but it was only me that could find his, while the light blinded him too much.

"That's not unusual in our scene at all. I think we have less monogamy than poly's, since our fetishes seldom are the same as whose form another person," the speaker explained, and I wondered why Deen hadn't mentioned it before since I literary struggled with accepting the fact of loving them both myself. Communication could have solved it all.

"It's not about love," Deen started, while Master Sattler nodded and continued, "I know, it doesn't have to be that either. In the vanilla word, you may have lived a seemingly normal, but for you, disappointing and unsatisfying life with just one person," he pointed out, and I wondered if this was the moment Deen learned to accept everything or if he just pretended to do so.

"Again, everybody, raise up your hands if you are poly," he requested, and I had to take mine up again. Even to me, it was a surprise that maybe 75% of the room did the same. I had imagined it to be almost half of the room, but that I was that normal here was very unusual, even to me, as I had talked to others at the BDSM meetings or parties before.

"That's insane. You make me feel like I am not a creep at all," Deen pointed out, and the entire room laughed even louder than they had been on the jokes of the speaker.

"About your fantasies, let us find some people who might have felt the same." Master Sattler was a good leader of the conversation and the programme itself. Easily, he engaged everybody in their conversation and opened up to talk about stigmatisations, problems, and unaccepted fantasies to open up a discussion and maybe even a kind of solution here and now.

"If we start with the one, I've heard most often from others but still assume as too extreme—extreme pain or even torture—with choking and giving the control fully into the hands of another person," his words surely touched at least half of the public's fantasies. Power dynamics are not seldom here, and to have them practiced with pain while one of them was a masochist and the other a sadist or a dominant thought about this as the best way to behold the line between the parts.

"All BDSM practitioners who may have fantasies involving intense pain or torture, such as needle play, extreme impact play, knife play, choking, or other types of breath control, raise your hands up," he demanded, and I almost couldn't see the stage anymore. It appeared like most of them had fantasies that were connected to any of the themes. Deen's mouth fell open, and afterwards they both laughed.

"Okay, next one, this was all too hard to choose just one of our dear Kinky communities to get onto the stage," the speaker said, and Deen nodded, still astonished that there were so many people who had the same fantasy, which he desperately had tried to subpress.

"While you always name and point out that all of the activities have to be consensual, there are some I have that don't appear to be alike." silence and waiting for what he wanted to say filled the room for some seconds. He swallowed deeply, while he missed eye contact with the publicum, but gave his attention to Master Sattler again.

"Both being and raping anybody, anywhere out of nowhere. Maybe even involved choking or really hard sex, while the victim desperately tries to come away." His words there were followed by a short applause, praising him for that he had told it to everybody, while the speaker patted him on the back before he continued to explain what this was in the kinky world.

"Consensual non-consent, also known as rape play, involves consensual role-playing scenarios where one partner temporarily gives up control and pretends to resist or be forced into sexual activity. It's not as uncommon as you think." Deen cut him off before he could ask for the people to raise their hands. "I am literary going to leave that room if half of the people are going to lift their hands up now too," he said in disbelief while the room and the speaker laughed.

"I think that it is not as common as the others, but you will see now; come on, everybody who fantasies about rape-play, lift up your hands," I said, and it took me a while to realize that Deen and I shared a lot of the same kinks, even if we had never talked about it. Deen himself laughed while he shook his head as many people raised their hands in the air. As the speaker had said, there were not that many who were convinced by the others, but still, at least 10% of the room had their hands raised up.

"Lusie, why did you never tell me?" he said in disbelief as he stepped off the stage to find anybody with the speaker to take up on it. I shrugged while I laughed. In the end, both I and another man got on the stage.

"Tell me, is this the girl you pointed out as "yours"?" Master Sattler asked Deen, and he nodded while he took my hand in his.

"Yes, this is Lusie, my girl, but also my best friend," he explained, avoiding the word brother, which may have led to confusion. I smiled and looked into his eyes only.
"Who are you then?" the speaker asked the man who sat beside me.

"My name is Borris, but I am surely better known as Master Blue in the scene," he explained, and some of the people in the audience laughed and cheered as he spoke. I hadn't seen him before, but already now I felt the room he took in for himself. Tall, broad-shouldered, military-like shaved, and hazel brown eyes, which were more intense than a firestorm, looked for a short second at me before they continued to talk again. I had hated myself before for feeling alike. Now, I had learned to accept it, while I still struggled with mentioning it, that somehow I had anything for very- dominant men in general. It had been Nathaniel who started the fire inside me, but the world he led me into was like hell, with a thousand thunderstorms and wild burning fires that caught my interest at once. Dangerous and bewildering, but I couldn't do anything against it.

"Okay, so we've got two switchers, each on the dominant or submissive side. What a good underground for a discussion about the theme," the speaker pointed out, and my body shivered at the thought of saying anything further on a stage in front of that many people.

"How to start such in the best way possible, with much communication or the RACK play-method, what do you think?" He asked, and all I knew was that I was thinking about whether everybody would look at me if I started to talk or if it would be seen as rare if I didn't say anything at all. The only thing that calmed me was Deen's comforting, warm hand on my upper leg, even if the thought that he did it because he was "taking" me as his own also came to mind. He had said it in front of everybody, so I inferred that this was the reason at first. On the other side, it could also be his natural instinct or that he had noticed my reaction, or, better yet, my affection, as the other man came to sit beside me. I didn't have a type of man that I liked most, if you had skin, hair, or eye colour in mind. For me, it was the aura that was most important. The way they captured much more space by just sitting normally on a chair. Like Nathaniel, affecting everybody in a surrounding area of a hundred meters. Master Blue was almost like that too, just much more aware of it. He played with it, and I wondered if that was a game I should continue to play or run away from. It could get dangerous, but wasn't that what a good game was built upon? Risk and wonder of what would happen if…

Chapter 5

"Excuse me, my girl and Deen would have to go with me. Now." My cool voice echoed through the room, even if I hadn't spoken loudly at all. Lusie smiled lightly, nodded politely, and went towards me, while Deen petrified me for a short while, in which he looked me in the eyes.

"Thank you for your attention to my story and help to figure out that I am almost normal here again," he said into the microphone, and after some laughter and applause, he would also follow me out.

"What happened?" they both asked me at once. We were there outside of the building.

What happened was better for me than at any other place. What should I say? I had waited for the discussion to take turns. Maybe the first time in my life I wasn't only afraid that something would happen to anybody I adored, but also that they would say it aloud. In front of everybody. Failure. Freek. Even worse is pettiness.

-     Why can't you have sex?

-     Do you have any illnesses?

-     Sorry that you had such a childhood.

"I needed to go," I said before the waiting for my response got rare, but as I went in front of them, hastily leading to my goal, my car, it might be hard not to think about my reaction as odd.

"Nathaniel, please wait," I heard Lusie begging, and in her voice, which I had only recognised once before. *"There is no way you can get me to any other place. I am not going away before we are the three of us again." "Why wouldn't he come back as he promised?"* I was here. Physical. Mentally, is another sake. However, there shouldn't be anything for her to worry about. Especially nothing that was related to somebody like me. Yes, I have accepted me with the edges of my past, but still, it was hard to never be enough for her. Even worse is not being able to do anything with it. Not alike Deen, who had taken the chance and got on the stage to get assured that his desire was normal in the scene.

I stopped and stood there in silence. I swallowed deeply before her hand touched my arm lightly. She tried to look me in the eyes, but they were fixed on my goal. Nobody could reach me right now. This wasn't a stadium you wanted to reach me at either.
"I love you," she whispered, and she slung her arms around me. For a second, I tensed even more and flexed my muscles, before somehow everything felt lighter. Like everything I had been worrying about was a primary nothing. Other, without any catch. It was almost rarely easy, so I started to think about whether it was possible to be like that.

Another hand touched my shoulder and squeezed it, but not as gently as Lusie did. It woke me from my dilemma of thoughts. They are not real. Nobody had said anything alike. It wasn't in their attention to hurt me in any way.

Lusie looked for a moment towards Deen before we all stood there, arms in arms. Holding each other while my pain ran away from the best moment that ever existed in my life. Not alone with Lusie, but as she always had wished, and now I wanted too, also with Deen.

In a small restaurant, we found ourselves twenty minutes later. The majority of visitors seemed to know each other or meet here usually, as they were chattering on a longer table.

There was a smaller table for exactly three people. It was round and stood beside a window. The number of plates that you had wasn't more than three, if each wanted to have a glass of water too.

"I like it here," Lusie pointed out as we sat down on the dark brown wooden chair. The fact that it was the same as how we sat, since we would sit beside everyone anyway, suited me. If I wanted them to talk about the event or have Lusie by my side while Deen was in front of us, He was on my left, while Lusie sat towards the window to my right.
"Have you anything in mind? What would you like to drink?" The older woman came to our table and asked us with a warm smile, which warmed the room at least as much as the old lamps, which were hanging very far down.

"Three waters," I said before anybody had the time to consider her question—Lusie didn't like to make decisions, and for Deen, it was easier than getting the thought of any sort of alcohol, which he might have chosen before.

"Okay, on my way." She was really on it before she had finished her sentence. You could see the years she had been spending here. Liking her job while not having more than enough for a living, even if she too had to work full time here. The world wasn't doing justice; following your passion could lead you to become a millionaire or the owner of a tiny restaurant, which you had to worry about each month to get around with the prizes. Often, these are the places that are not too expensive.

"What do you think about taking the first step and talking about a constellation of ways our relationship could work together?" Lusie was more positive and enthusiastic about figuring that out than usual. since we had been at the event right now and got explained how such could work alike and what you had to take care of. She didn't use the internet, so this was the most informative evening she had in years.

"Isn't it quite simple, since we do have every part twice?" Deen said, referring to himself as being each part once, while Lusie was only being submissive, and I remained just dominant too.

"It can be, if you're fine with it," I said, and he looked for a second at me, not knowing exactly what I was referring to. The fact that I wasn't going to be "under" him did take amusingly long for him to take in.

"Okay, for summing your idea up as I have understood it, you "own" the both of us, while I can also play with Lusie as her dominant." He figured it out, and after a short hesitation, I nodded. Even if I hadn't said it like that, it was, in the end, the same as what I had in mind.

"Just to make it clear, we aren't going to have anything aside from the power dynamic." Deen pointed between the two of us, and Lusie started to laugh, while I raised an eyebrow, wondering what he was referring to. Me, who is not able to have any sexual intercourse, having penetrability sex with him or her, which may be bisexual, but still somebody I know since I was six years old, doing anything alike to me, for saying it the child-friendly way.

"It won't be any problem. I just have to know your boundaries and desires," I said with a raised eyebrow, while he nodded hastily, almost ashamed of his thoughts. Nobody had to be that; it wasn't anything I wanted to reach with it either. I just didn't understand him. That was something I didn't appreciate at all—not understanding what anybody meant, was referring to, or felt while sitting beside me.

"Here's your water; do you have anything in mind for dinner?" both looked at me, and I got aware that their 24/7 power dynamic mainly meant that I also took decisions they didn't want to make. An example is deciding what we all would eat on a Friday afternoon, which was both healthy and nutritious.

"We'll take the fried vegetable rice with chicken," she nodded with a smile and went away again. Again, there were just the three of us on one table, which meant that we didn't sit far away at all. If we all slid more in, our knees would touch under the table, and you never knew what would happen under such a top.

"Sorry for that, I went on stage today." Deen excused himself, and my first intention was to assure him that there was nothing to apologise for. There wasn't anything either, but still, it would have been a lie if I said that it hadn't affected my small "breakdown" outside afterwards.

"We're good," I assured him with a smile, while I just looked into his eyes, since it was something for him to understand what I had been feeling about it. Even if Deen wasn't good at reading others, I could tell that he understood what I meant right now—without that action, we wouldn't sit here like this now and discuss the next step.

As a move that could lead us further, but also back again. Like this, it was always about starting new dynamics while having other ideas. The most important thing you have to keep in mind is never to give up. If you step forward, but anything throws you two steps back, you have to run forward again before it catches you. We have to move on. Remaining like that wouldn't be a good long-term thought.

Chapter 6

You should start to eat less, or else you aren't going to fit to throw the door in a few weeks." I was kidding with Deen while I laughed out loud. He needed another portion in addition to eating the rest of mine.

"I am a hard-working man now, so keep caring about that tiny mouth of yours, not that you aren't going to be a hard-working woman tonight too." Deen teased me, and like that, I was it too, but Nathaniel reacted a little badly to the fact.

"Keep care about what leaves your mouth, or you are going to wish that you ever would be able to take out the trash again." We both didn't stop, and even if he didn't mean it 100% seriously, he had meant it way more alike than we had been, while we were teasing ourselves about all too much. Sex work was well nothing to laugh about in front of Nathaniel; that was understandable, but still something that I had to remind myself of more often, especially while I was as relaxed as now and didn't think about what left my mouth at all.

"Big words, no action. Dear brother, I wondered if you would ever be able to dominate me at all. At least I am not scared to try to prove you." For a while, I stopped to smile and looked between the two of them, wondering what would happen now. Deen had a challenging smile on his lips, while Nathaniel looked at him but didn't show any emotions at all. The familiar mask made me wonder if he was upset or figuring out if he would "accept" the challenge.

"I give you ten seconds to put these clothes on and stand in front of me. Naked. Powerless. Waiting for whatever I will do to you," his words would have cut through the air if the pleasure hidden in it hadn't made my body shiver and a smile appear on my lips. I liked his playful side, and yes, that was it. It was the start of a so-called session, the first we had with the three of us.

"Lusie, help him," my name made me jump at once on the way to him. I wasn't a person who would try to get away from or around any commands. I accepted them at once. In "real life," I had learned that, here, I didn't see any point in provoking my dominant in any way.

As Deen was completely naked in front of the two of us, I came into a rare situation. My cheeks turned red, but I wasn't used to seeing an undressed male body. My own had become familiar to me, but that didn't mean that it was the same with others. Where should I look now? What should I do? Before the questions ate me up, the next order came. Hard. Exact. Without any room for complaints.
"Show them that he doesn't deserve that mouth of yours. Don't make him come"—two s sentences that made me kneel down while Deen looked down at me with a sly smile. He may have liked his brother's idea, but I could imagine that there would be more. Nathaniel had just started, and once the fire was made, it would burn for a while.

He didn't wait, nor did he stare at us. Calmly, he took off his jacket and placed it beside the door. A short glance at us, and then nothing again. Like he didn't care at all, he went to the sleeping room and didn't return for surely two minutes.

As he came, he was dressed in black jeans and a leather jacket, which looked even better on him than his normal outfits. He recognised that I was mainly looking at him while he was near us and went to me with a gentle smile to streak a hair out of my face. I am never looking at Deen or anything else but me in this minute. "Stop now. Undress yourself. Deen," he said his name, and while his brother cursed for that, I had to halt.

"You go into the sleeping room and lay yourself on the bed with your bed facing towards the matrass." Another position wouldn't have been possible in his primary condition either. Without a second word, he went away and left me with Nathaniel in the garage department of the apartment.

Before I would or could say anything, he stood beside me. Slowly, I raised my tiny body, in comparison to his, so that I stood there at my full height too. Still, my head wasn't even over his shoulders.

"You do what I say. If I say that you hit him, you hit him. If I say that you fuck him, you fuck him. If I say that you choke him, Before he could finish his sentence, I did it for him. "I'll choke him." A light smile appeared on his lips, and he stepped even closer. Not a paper blad would have been fitting between us at this moment.

"Exactly. Good girl," his hand touched my chin softly while the other one stoked my nipple barely. I exhaled sharply at the surprising touch. A satisfied smile crossed his lips before he left me again. Wet. Hard nipples. I long for his touch and warmth, which I was missing.

"Follow me while you look down on the ground. Nowhere else, before I allow it." His wish was my command, and so I went after him, while my eyes never pointed anywhere but, on the ground, while an excited smile rested on my lips.

I didn't see anything, but I heard anything getting looked up. Like a door or... handcuffs. I had seen them before, but Jake wouldn't use them often on me. He preferred "real" bondage, as he said. It didn't matter to me; I liked both the same way.
"Look up, little girl, and see what you have done to him. Helpless. Extradite to me. Imagine that I could kill him. Hurt or torture him in front of you; without that, you would be able to do anything." It wasn't about the event itself. We all knew that it wasn't going to happen and that nobody wanted it to go on. It wasn't about that, not at all. More the fact of unhelplessness. I trusted him so much that he might do everything he wanted to you, but as it was still the same person, I was sure that he wouldn't do it in the end. Playing with ideas and imaginations of what it would be like to stand there, not able to do anything. For Deen, how the pain would feel and the touches of the belt or whatever Nathaniel preferred to use. Never had he harmed me in any way before, and I wondered if he was even the right person for such a thing. Even if he himself had a powerful presence, he would never use it against anyone. I reminded myself that this was for our pleasure, not against anyone.

Still, playing with pain wasn't anything I could put myself into. Too much had happened before in the real world, so this might never lead to any kind of pleasure for me.

"Make love to him." Nathaniel whispered, but before I saw the order in it, I turned around once again to find a crying man behind me. Not sobbing, but just a small tear gliding down his cheeks while he watched the two of us. Both naked, he bent to the bed, each leg and arm spread to the corners of the bed, while I just stood there in front of it. Not knowing what would be right to do or if it would turn out to be my first obedience. Seeing him like that inched into every piece of me, especially my heart. Still, remembering his words, which were haunting the other part of me. *You do what I say. If I say that you hit him, you hit him. If I say that you fuck him, you fuck him. If I say, You choke him,"* "I'll choke him," my reply, which had sounded like it was an easy thing to do, still I wasn't sure if I ever was able to do anything alike.

It wasn't like with Jake. With him, it was, in a way, "just" him. Even if I hadn't anything against him and even liked his person very much, it was nothing in comparison to the brothers. Here, it felt like each step I took could lead into a dark, deep hole for at least one of us, and the risk wasn't anything erotic for me at all. Love wasn't easy. BDSM wasn't easy. Nathaniel wasn't easy, and neither were Deen or I. Still, we wanted this and worked towards it. If it never did, we would at least have tried. Already, at the beginning of everything, I could tell that it wouldn't be easy, even if both of them were not giving up. Not once, as we have started now. However, there were not just two in this relationship; there were three. I would also have my word to say, and even if I didn't name it "giving up," I would have to put a stop to it. Now. Before it got too late, or I did anything I or anybody else would regret at the end of the day,.

"Red," the word that was easy and short, had more meaning in itself than some of the longest books I had been reading. Red wasn't just a colour or a stop signal; it also symbolised the desire to reach something in a controlled way. Maybe I was overthinking the situation, but if I was not, I would never forgive myself for letting it happen. It was my right as a sub to stop everything any time I wished. Jake had assured me several times that it was smart to not be scared of doing that if I felt bad, everything got too much for me, or anything didn't feel like it should.

The last statement referred to our action. He shouldn't be crying. I can't remember having seen that any other time before. Tears were flooding silently down his chin, a rarity he never showed anybody whom he didn't trust. This is what we had to do to each other here. However, to believe in each other meant also to take care of each other, which I would do now. Nothing else mattered, just the wellbeing of everyone.

Deen looked up in shock at once the words had left my mouth, thinking that there was anything wrong with him, but at once he looked for a second towards Nathaniel; he knew why I had been saying it. It wasn't a loss; it was a new start and taught all of us that we have to be comfortable with whatever we are doing, seeing, saying, or hearing. He didn't have to do that, but yet he wanted us to make love to each other, maybe to see if hearts and flowers would cover the mood in the room afterwards. Nobody wanted that. Hearts there read as blood, and flowers could be any other organ in our body. That wasn't how our relationship would work. We already loved each other. There was no need to say it or show it over and over again and again. Now, we could have fun and pleasure and discover our desires in every single way, while we all had to be fine with it. Crossing borders was one thing, not helping the other one back again.

Chapter 7

Sadness can be likened to a shadow that lingers in the corners of the soul, a silent witness to the depths of human experience. It emerges not as a mere absence of joy but rather as a profound echo of past wounds, a testament to the complexities of existence. Like a gentle breeze stirring the leaves of a tree, sadness whispers the stories of our pain and longing, weaving a tapestry of emotions that shape our perception of the world. It is a reminder of our capacity to feel, to empathise, and to connect with others in the shared journey of life. What happens if you isolate yourself and never talk to your friends or at least a professional about it? He hadn't lost control over us; he had gone over his own boundaries while trying to give us the pleasure he imagined we wanted. At this point, he was missing something; there was only pleasure and joy existing for the three together. Seeing him like this was a call of having gone too far. Lusie had recognised it. Hopefully not too late...

"Nathaniel, are you?" she started to say while going towards him. Have you ever seen raindrops turn into ice? You see that the water has existed, but since it's frozen down, it isn't that literary anymore. Like this, he seemed to disappear in some way. Going towards me instead of accepting the care from her. Running away, he could now, but there were two to catch him, and he wouldn't do that again. Ever. Falling in our arms was one thing, but running away each time it got complicated was another. Trust wasn't easy, but we all had to believe in each other for this to work. There was no other option.

"I am fine," he said, cutting her off while he already stood beside me and loosened the handcuffs from the bed. Once I was free, I almost jumped up against him.

"You are **not** going to do that. Ever. Again. Have you heard me? It is not about doing what you think we would like; it is more about what you accept and want from us. " I pointed at the situation before I searched his eyes again.
"Was a lesson for the three of us on how we shouldn't do it? I am not going to provoke you, but you are not going to make us do anything you cannot appreciate to see." My words were there colder than I had meant them to be. A warning for a storm was in the room under our skins but slowly became visible.

"You are not my dominant, and if you think that it harms me to see you two having pleasure, you are completely wrong. The only thought that is unbearable is that I am not able to do it myself. I am working on it. On myself, every day and time. Still, it is not easy. I need time to be able to do all that myself." His words were not as expected; they were as strong as they came from a bear. He decided, knowing what he wanted from us in every way. What I didn't like was the way he referred to himself. He wasn't of any importance at all. It was just about Lusie's and my pleasure. There was no way he would be able to have it now by himself.

"If you don't even try, I am out, and I can tell you, Lusie too. We both aren't narcissistic. The pleasure of a session should belong to the three of us." My words were clear, like my idea, but he did nothing. Not even a hint of a change of expression. Like they never existed, just a hallucination of my own. For a short second, I turned towards Lusie, but she was also just waiting for him to talk. We were both there, standing there, me still all naked, just inches away from Nathaniel. She was also undressed, but further away.

"Take a shower. You two. Now," he turned after he had said this around like the safeword had never been used. I was her dom too. I could also assure me that she was fine. May it even help us to form a deeper bond? Still, I wanted him to do that. He was the person who always led everything in my life and never made any kind of mistake. What was that now? Did I have a reason to check after him and ask her instead of our dominant if everything was okay?

Confusion about what the right thing to do was spread itself in me. In silence, we went to the shower. He had disappeared; he was still anywhere in the apartment, but nowhere for us to be seen. "Are you alright?" I asked Lusie as soon as we had closed the door behind us. "Yes, it was not about me that I stopped. I feared doing anything wrong or harming him while doing what he asked for, while seeing his teary eyes," she explained, and I gave her a kiss on her forehead for the sweat statement. If it had been the best thing to do, we might never get to know, but the fact that it felt right made sense that this wouldn't matter. Doing anything that your heart is already telling you not to do before you even take a step towards it might never be a good thing to do. Stepping over your own borders can be done, but you will always need somebody to track you back into safety again. Especially if there is any point where you want to harm yourself, like Nathaniel may have wanted.

"Come here, darling." I let her burry her face into my chest while the warm water fell on us. Thousands of water drops, like on a warm summer night, aside from the fact that we almost had December. Outside, there was almost no sun anymore, just rain and snow on the colder days of the year. In a few days, we may have to stay at the clinic if it gets too much of the white substance in front of the door. I wasn't sure if I looked forward to it or tried not to think about how our alone time here could ever end.

"I have found an apartment close to your clinic; should we take a look at it by tomorrow?" Nathaniel greeted us sincerely as we went out of the bathroom. I frowned, stopped, and looked at him in silence for a few seconds until I realised that he did mean that it might be smart if Lusie and I had our own place.

"Are you kidding with me?" I asked in disbelief while I stepped toward him, until we almost touched.

"You want to throw us out, because" he cut me off in the middle of my sentence, shaking his head and balling his fists together, like this wasn't an easy conversation for him to have.

"I am not throwing anybody out here. Just thinking that it might be better if I was." I shook my head now too, while I cut him off. If he was thinking that would make anything better, he was completely wrong. Usually, he wasn't a person to run away from his problems, which showed me the deep mark that remained in his soul.

"Listen to me now; we are going to stay here or move together. There is no way that you are getting rid of me or Lusie, especially after such an event. If you haven't understood it yet, she loves you, while she loves me too. I don't want to see her suffering from heartbreak, especially if I was able to stop the event." He wanted to cut my monologue off again, but I raised a hand for him to stay silent.

"You can let us go throw this together or push us away for playing the mooning swan. Whatever you choose, we are going to be there for you. Just know one thing." I stopped for a while, letting the silence stay between us while I leant forward so that only he could hear me.

"While harming yourself, you also hurt us. We are one. If one of us is in pain, we are all sharing it so that it gets easier for this part. We are a body out of three pieces; if anything doesn't function, the others have to help it, since there would be a large missing piece without it. If one part feels pain, it will be everywhere else too. Do you understand what I mean?" I stepped a little out of his private zone again, looking him deeply into the eyes. An amusing smile was shadowed on his lips, and I wondered if that was a good sign or just anything that showed me that he wasn't accepting nor hearing anything I had said. I like making fun of it. Which I dwelled upon, since he never had wanted to damage me in any way, and if that would be the case, it would hurt.

"I love you too, little brother." His word hit me a little out of nowhere, but as I was thinking back on what I had been saying, I understood what it really was.

Something that I always had pushed away and never wanted to admit. Sleeping with hundreds of girls instead to make sure that it was out of the realm of reality. Imagine that it never left the deepest part of me. Who could know that it might not only be brotherly love that lingered inside me? I didn't know what it was either. Just that it could be wonderful and the most painful feeling I had ever felt at once. Too deep to run away from, but too good to want to do that too. Bisexual. Like he always said. I never understood that it was me he was referring to, not himself. The world fell hardly at my feet. It was enough for a lifetime to consider. Accepting BDSM, love, sexuality, traumas, and feelings was, well, at least more than enough for a day.

Chapter 8

Days had passed, even weeks had gone over quickly. Still, they hadn't blamed me once for the event which happened that Friday night. They should do that. I did it. I had always kept thinking that a good dominant would never hear the safeword out of his sub's mouth. While I had thought about their feelings, I had ignored my own. Sad enough that I was relaxing there too much, so that my mask fell on the floor, and my real emotion appeared. I hated feelings; they had never helped me in any way before, would only stop me off or make others worry about nothing. How many times did I have to assure Lusie that I was fine before she could relax again. How many times did I have to smile, just for that she would do the same again too. And how many times did I have to put on a mask beside her, just that nobody, especially Lusie, wouldn't start to worry about my well-being.

"You want to come with me today too?" I looked at her, as she took on herself a jacket as I wanted to head to Deen's clinic.

"Tell me why I should be alone here the entire day, while just the two of you are working. Always thought about you as a modern man; can you imagine that I, as a woman, cannot sit still the entire day either?" that she challenged me was new, but maybe just because she didn't want to give me the chance to let her here alone.

With every power she had she wanted to join me, as we head to many people which might could lose their control every second. I did not like that thought…

There we sat again, as a couple in my car. In just some minutes I would tense as hell, while seeing all whose strangers, which potentially could harm her. May they would not today or tomorrow either, but I didn't like the constant risk. I didn't like risks at all. Sick got healthy, not maybe, it had to get this. Else I would never have opened a clinic which almost assured my patients to a hundred percent that they would leave it as they are and not with a black car with a cross above.

"Why do you not like me by your side anymore?" she asked me out of the sudden, and as I had to concentrate on the road, I couldn't look at her. Still, I frowned. Where did that idea come from? I had never said or showed anything alike. May I had gotten more distant, but that was just for her own safety. I had lost control about myself once. Not for her, but for me to harm. It should not happen again, yet I could only stop it out with not trying it again. At least if I wanted to be a hundred percent sure about that it would **never** happen again.

"I do not" I said simply, and as the traffic got lighter looked toward her for two seconds. While she looked out on the other side, not showing me what she felt by a hint of the look into her eyes.

"You are not the same in the last two weeks. You got distanced, not only in the way you try to avoid any kind of touches, but also with your head. You have never been that before" her words made me shiver in horror. I didn't like that she convinced me with myself and said that I had changed. There was a lot which did happen. The justice wasn't longer than three weeks ago. Still, there was a lot to take in, even if she was right with that my "abstinence" didn't come therefrom. I wouldn't say anything to her. She worried already and would only assure me over and over again that it was fine.

"There is a lot to think about" I said simply, thinking that it might would stop her from relating everything to herself and Deen. May they there the reason, not the case or how I should continue my living. Right now, it was mainly them. Stupid enough, since I did not come a step further in my own life, while just helping Deen each day for free.

"If you don't start talking to me, I will literary track you to an psychologise" she said offended and I started to smile in amusement, in mind her while she tried to pull me anywhere to anybody. I would **not** go. Ever. Pity and shock from others I had grown tired of as a child already, as I had to tell each from the youth welfare further times what had happened. They even wanted to punish my mother for it, but already then, I had said that it was not her fault. With six years I had understood, what many people don't understand their entire life's.

"I would love you trying, but I don't like seeing you failing. Therefore, don't do it" I said firmly, not showing a hint of my smile anymore. I heard her taking a deep sight, but before she could say anything more, we had already pulled into the parking lot of Deen's clinics.

"Good morning" I greeted Deen at first, so that Lusie hadn't the chance to comment anything which had been discussed in the car. I knew that this wasn't over, but I didn't appreciate it to continue here.

"Better mood today? Good morning to you too" he looked at me sceptically, and I wondered which types of mood-swinging's he was referring to. From saying nothing to a good morning, while beholding the same kind of expression the entire time? Good way to start at.

"You can help me with a patient today, Lusie" Deen said at once she entered the room, and I stiffened.
"She is not..." I started, trying to say how unhappy I was with the thought of seeing her anywhere close to anybody in this house. IN my clinic it would never have been any kind of problem. Here it was. Neither did I knew who his patients where, nor are they known as simple to handle or estimate.

"I will be there all the time. Don't worry. I have also a lot for you to do" very pleasant. My younger brother telling me what to feel...

"If you lose her for one second, even if nothing happens" I almost threatened him, while he rolled his eyes and took on his doctor clothing.

"I am not going to. Relax here. We'll be back in about half an hour" he informed me, and they both let me behind like they wouldn't mind about my dwellings at all. No further comments, assurances or polite thanking's for my worry. Nothing. Like they didn't care. Like I just was a worker here.

That game wouldn't last long, definitely if he started to play it against me in any kind of way. There are many other things which I definitely would prefer to do over his paperwork. I did it for him since he would have more time off with us then. However, if he acted alike, it wasn't assured that I wanted to spend much more time with him. I would also like to start everything again of my own, which I could now, since there was nobody which stood in my back anymore.

After the case, they had tokened the pharmacists with themselves, and he would spend the rest of his lifetime from now on in prison. Not only that, also he had to get lessons about human worth, equality and even start to write apologies to **every single** person which had token the untested medicamentation or been a victim in any other way. In prison, I thought, he would surely have a lot of time for that.

"Excuse me?" one of his nurses entered the door. I remembered her exactly – Stella Stowell, she was our first interview. The one I thought he was lucky with, after many other with equal qualifications came one after one.

"Yes?" I looked at her and wondered if there already had been anything between my brother and her. Not that it would be my problem, even if I had said to him further times that staff was off limit. However, his clinic, meant that it was also his responsibility. As long as he did make sure that she was taking birth control or he used a condom, I hadn't to consider the fact anymore, than just for that second.

"Could you help me with a patient?" she asked shily, and I stood up at once. I would never have started a clinic alike that. It was all too dangerous and inestimable.

"Of course, I am on my way. What's the problem?" I asked directly, while I took a doctor coat over my clothes, so that everyone would see my qualifications. It made it at least easier. Somehow some people still thought that a doctor only was a doctor with that clothing.

"The patient is unconscious, even if there is not any reason for that" she explained, and several possibilities came to my mind.

As we went into the room, she had been talking about. The patient still lay there on the bed without any sense of awakens. Slowly I went to him, while I scanned his body from head to feet. I went throw the first five possibilities which came to my mind;

1. Severe withdrawal symptoms, which means that withdrawal symptoms can be extremely intense, leading to a significant physiological response. Severe symptoms such as seizures or delirium tremens can result in loss of consciousness.

2. Dehydration and electrolyte imbalance. Throughout the withdrawal, symptoms can lead to dehydration and electrolyte imbalances in the body, which can affect brain function and lead to unconsciousness.

3. Hypoglycaemia, means that some individuals may experience low blood sugar levels during their withdrawal. Particularly if they have not been eating properly or if their substance use has affected their diet.

4. Other Health Complications, like that the individual may has underlying health issues that are exacerbated by the stress of withdrawal, potentially leading to unconsciousness.

5. Or the psychological distress of withdrawal which also can contribute to unconsciousness. Extreme anxiety, panic attacks, or other mental health issues can sometimes lead to loss of consciousness.

"What is he diagnosed with?" I asked her while she stood unhelpful behind me, totally scared of that there was anything serious with the patient, while I made quick checks of the vitals.

"Just the alcohol after his wife's car accident. Nothing more" she assured me, but I already had figured out the problem before she had explained the unhelpful tip.

"He hasn't eaten enough" I said and she shook her head while she assured me that he had been eating in the clinics small restaurant every single day. Naïve she was definitive. If she would have token a look at the thinning hair, brittle nails, dry and yellowish skin, while the person definitely was under the average wight, she have recognized his anorexia.

"He is totally dehydrated, typical for his secondary sickness. He needs enteral nutrition at once he is awake again, but at first just water. Make it slowly, don't overfill him at once. That is not going to help" I warned her while she hurried out of the room to get the devices we needed.

"Good work, miss Stowell" I praised her while the patients slowly wakened, and a shy smile covered her face. Her reaction had after my diagnosis been very quick. I couldn't say anything against that. She may should have figured it out by herself, but I forgave her that, considering that she was in shock.

"Get anybody to check him every fifteen minutes, then he is fully awake again, out can start with the food" I said quickly, and stood after I had token several checks for the third time, up again to leave. She followed me, why I didn't ask. Neither did I turn around, or she say anything toward me. However, at once I came into the office, I had to role my eyes. She appeared shortly after me, and at once she saw Deen while he kissed Lusie deeply, I heard her flinch and disappear behind me. There this man would get some problems. That I could tell already. He hadn't touched her before, even if she was **very** open for further interactions with him. It was almost that I thought about her as a poor girl, since she would see him almost every single day further times, without getting real abstinence from the clinic, since she lived here too.

Chapter 9

"Your family did not know anything about it?" I asked the girl in my age, whom Deen had brought me too, since she, for religious reasons, didn't want a man to touch her. Not even a doctor. However, with the alcohol, she had not seen any end, even if, as much as I knew, Muslims shouldn't drink that either.

"Of course not. I knew it was wrong, but there was some kind of thrill behind it. Additionally, I really liked him," she said the last words silently. As she explained her story there, she had started to hang with a guy after school. Her parents thought that she was with some of her female friends. Since they are very conservative, she didn't want them to know anything about either of the two forbidden things she did in their eyes. With the alcohol, she'd told me, she wouldn't start before they told her about the arranged marriage that they had been planning for her. The guy just helped her get it, even if he didn't know anything about the reason for the sudden mind-change.

"Have you ever told them that you are not interested in marrying the other man?" I wondered if my questions were too many, but she answered each of them, and I was really curious.

"Are you insane? They would have killed me or threw me out of the family if I didn't obey our traditions," her eyes wide in shock at my unhelpful idea. It sounded most logical to me, but as I didn't know much about it, probably it wasn't the best idea.

"Take this around her upper arm now," Deen commanded, as he had not the permission of her to neither do nor look upon her like that.

"Turn around," she commanded him again, as he wanted to see if I was placing the blood pressure tape right. He raised his arms and did what he wanted. Even if I dwelled on the idea that this would be a smart idea of hers, I had to remind myself that it wasn't hers but her family's, which wanted this too.

"What have you said to them about where you are now?" I asked her, and she began, all of a sudden, to cry.

"I have not said anything at all. They don't know it. I just have to get healthy again as soon as possible. Alone, I have tried, but the presence of alcohol is everywhere. In every store, friends housing, or while you just go alongside the road and see people drinking in the evening," she tried to stop her tears with the other hand, but they would just slide away beside it and drop down on her clothes. I gave her, therefore, a handkerchief, which lay on the desk beside me. She took it thankfully, but her tears wouldn't stop anyway. Her body didn't obey her; all too much was the weight she had to bear. Someday, even the highest walls you have built as protection are going to not be enough for the water that builds up behind them.

"We would be very pleased to help you in any way. If there is anything, just say it, alright?" I asked her, and she nodded with a thankful smile.

"You could contact my friend and tell him where I am. I would love to have him here," she explained, and I started to wonder if that would be a good idea since her parents could technically also arrive. On the other hand, she was eighteen, and according to the law, she was a grownup. They couldn't stop their love, and neither should they if they didn't want to lose their daughter. I couldn't imagine why they would prefer their religion before their own flesh and blood.

"Deen, what are you doing?" I giggled. Once the doors had closed behind us, he couldn't take his hands off me. Somehow Nathaniel wasn't here waiting for us, but that didn't matter in this second. Warm hands everywhere under my clothes, while our mouths found each other.

Longing for the touches and beautiful feelings, while we had nobody else but the two of us in mind. At least until the door opened, catching us out of nowhere.

"Nathaniel," I said after some heartbeats, and understanding came to my mind about the fact that he should have been here but was not. He was free to move everywhere in the building, but he still didn't like to be between "dangerous" people, as he had referred to them. I didn't feel the same about that; they wanted to come away from the substance that had ruined their lives; why should they harm anybody else's then?

He looked behind himself for a second, while Deen and I got a little more distant from each other.

"You may have some problems with one of your employees," he said after closing the doors. Deen frowned, not understanding why he would know that now where he had been and which worker he was talking about.

"Stella Stowell is completely fallen for the blond prince in doctor's coat," he said ironically about everything, except the first part. I didn't know who she was, nor would I care if Deen would have anything with her too, but as it took him out of the shock, I knew he did not.

"Why is this going to lead him to any kind of problem?" I asked while I went closer to Nathaniel, which still tracked me towards him like a magnet with just being there. His presence wasn't compatible with anybody else's. More intense, and everything I wanted described in one person—aside from the polygamy.

"I have recognised that she was very willing to work more often than the others. Her job, she did well, and also the others she took optional; they were perfectly finished," Deen explained while he shrugged, like he did not care much about her feelings. Turning away from us again and sitting down to do some more work, like nothing had happened.

"Not to be impolite, but would you care why I am wearing that coat, which I dislike with my entire heart?" Nathaniel tried to make Deen more attentive. Slowly, without any sense of haste, he turned around and looked at his brother from head to toe.

"Why are you wearing the prince's coat, since you want me to ask?" After a rolling of his eyes, he explained about the unconscious of one of his patients, which made Deen jump up before he even finished telling what really had happened.

There we stood, left alone. Not me and Deen alone in one room anymore, but Nathaniel instead. I should get furious too, but somehow, I was just glad to spend time with them both. After more than just a few minutes, we had achieved the hour count.

"Was everything fine with that patient you and Deen visited?" he asked me, and I nodded at once while remembering her story, which truly touched my heart. Being constantly under the control of your parents under the control of your parents for the rest of your life didn't seem like anything I wanted to have, and in a way, I luckily could not either.

"She is my age and a Muslim. Started to drink after getting to know that she has to have an arranged marriage while loving another guy." I explained the short version for him, but he just nodded like it was totally normal.

"I am not religious in any way myself; therefore, it might be hard to judge their behaviour out of my atheistical purpose." His rational answers would someday kill me. Wasn't he able to show any sympathy for the poor girl? Didn't he have any feelings for her story at all? How would that be possible? We humans feel anything for everything while we judge it after what we know, with affection for our emotions towards it.

"Be kind, and don't hang yourself too much up to all that. You never know what else is playing a role in another person's life. Imagine what others think about us, or when I call Deen my brother. There is always a lot that happened behind the scenes, and nobody else will ever get to know anyway," he read me again like a book as I stood there with widening eyes, my smile for once faded.

"Maybe you're right, but still, it's cruel to think about. I kind of wonder what I would have done in her position." He turned fully around to face me again. In his eyes, I saw honesty, while he was a little tensed and maybe even a little worried.

"Don't waste your time on anybody who wouldn't give you a second of his own to do anything for you. She has another life, purpose, dreams, and point of view in our society. Nobody will know everything about any person. Especially not we, as strangers, are able to make a judgement about that. Keep in mind that nobody else but yourself is ever going to take advantage of what you want to achieve. Beside me, of course," he smiled and turned around again, while I let his words sink in. In the end, we will all be alone. Whatever we have done for others is of no importance while our own lives are over.

Chapter 10

“I am finished now. We can go,” Deen said as he put on his normal clothing while we prepared everything for the next day.

“Good to go then." Nathaniel turned towards me, and I smiled immediately. Just to symbolise that I am fine and also ready to go.

“When are we going to start to drive for an hour just so that you don’t take us to the same restaurants over again?” Deen asked simply as Nathaniel wrote in the address for our today’s restaurant.

"Never.” His answer made me laugh, wondering if he already had some backup plans or if we were going to move to another place anytime soon. I liked the garage, since it brought us even closer together. Not because it was small, but since there was only one sleeping option for the three of us. It may have been rare, but that suited me very well.

“Is it Asia today?” he referred to the type of restaurant while Nathaniel had an amusing smile on his lips. It was the weekend; taking a break didn’t exist in the private medicine world. Then you owned a clinic that was always open; you also had to be there and prepare everything for both your patients and employees. Of course, they could contact Deen if anything unexpected happened, but that should be more of a backup plan than normality.

"Italian, I like that idea," Deen said at once as we drove into the tiny parking lot in front of the small restaurant. They mainly delivered, but they also had view tables and chairs inside. Though it looked very old from the outside, the interior was a mixture of modern and vintage.

While Nathaniel ordered the food for us, we went to one of the tables.

"What do you think? Where will we be in five years, or you in particular? What are you working on too? Or do you think we will have enough restaurants in our closer surroundings that we can make the same each single day?" Deen laughed at my sudden questions while he clearly started to think about the main one. It wasn't easy to think that long into the future. Especially if you are there not just thinking about you but about others lives that are connected with yours.

"Even though the garage is fine, I would like to have a real house instead. It doesn't have to be a villa; I would also like that we had in Croatia at the Lakes," I laughed as he pointed out. We didn't have anything there except a bed and bathroom. Enough for two persons of romantic space; we had to get over that line.

"Or like Jake's house, but I wouldn't want to have it that big, and with this count of sleeping rooms," he laughed for a moment, while the mood changed in a way. Jake. He was away. We would never see him again, as he had said to me. Yet the time spent with him, we will never forget. It had been special. He was special. He was very interested in getting us closer to one another, while his own "relationship" had failed while I was there. It had been the first time I was actually a little afraid of him too.

"What about your clinic? Has anything changed?" I asked him while his eyes widened, and he clearly had to consider at first what he wanted to have in the future and what this was doable in the next few years.

"Don't understand me wrong; I like it like it is right now. On the other hand, I know that Nathaniel is almost in need of starting his business again too. As I have a large building and outdoor area, I would like him to make something together with me. I don't have to be the owner of everything. Just my withdrawal department is of any importance for me, while he wants to help the entire world if he could," Deen explained honestly, and I wondered what the problem was that lay behind it. The case was over, and they already had the building. Maybe it was the "sort" of people who would come together. Even if I thought about whose at Deen's clinic as normal people, which just had not tokened the right turn for once.

"What are you talking about?" Nathaniel came back again, with a raised eyebrow, in wonder of where our conversation had led us too.

"About you starting a larger company at Deen's clinic with further departments of clinical treatments for several sicknesses," I explained the last part, which seemed to be in a way important to Deen. Even if he wanted to succeed himself, he wasn't blind to the feelings of others. He wasn't able to read him like Nathaniel, which made it easy. No, he just noticed as much as I had that Nathaniel hadn't been in any relaxed mood the past few weeks; maybe since the "accident," he had stopped to think about his own feelings altogether. We wanted him to be fine again, but there was no option to do anything without that; he wanted it. He wouldn't appreciate it. Even if it was against our best will, maybe he would say that he was already used to doing everything by himself, which made it wasn't helpful for him if we tried to do anything for him the entire time.

"One day, why not?" he said after he had been thinking about it for a few seconds, and Deen's face lit up.

"You really mean it? Are we working together for a giant clinic?" he asked more enthusiastically, hoping to fill his voice.

"There are possibilities; we never know where the future will lead us. It could be something to work forward to," he explained, like we were there talking about a game, not live. Easily. Considered. Powerful, as always.

"What would I do in your great company? The cleaning?" I teased them while they both rolled their eyes in seemingly the same second afterwards.

"No way," it almost looked like they had rehearsed everything since it happened in the same second; without that, they looked at each other.

"What about you becoming a doctor? In five years, you could work for us too in the department of your choice," he explained while I laughed about it as if it were a joke. Before, I had the grades but never the time or money to study anything anywhere. I was just born to work. Never had I considered my passion anything else beside that.

"One day, surely a year ago, you said that you had been reading my medical books in my abstinence, so why not, if you are interested in the theme?" It shocked me as Nathaniel too started with it. Now, everything seemed more serious, and for the first time ever, I started to wonder how it would be to work in their clinic as a doctor, like they are too.

I liked the fact that I would see the both of them both at work and in our spare time, but I wondered if it was a good idea to make everything together all the time too. There was a possibility that everything would end, even if I dwelled upon it and did not at all want it. However, humans changed as much as their dreams, wishes, wants, and goals. If we would include one another in each theme in five years, was a large question that wasn't possible to answer before this count of time had passed. We could consider what was most likely now, but we were not able to make a clear decision for ourselves in many years. Even I didn't know how I would think about it in the future. Right now, I was just sure that there was nothing I could be happier with than staying together as the trio we are.

"I don't know if I am able to do that." I referred to the medicine study, which was not only very long but also one of the hardest.

"If it is your past grades you worry about, that isn't going to be any problem. Ask Deen. Everything else aside, I am very sure that you are going to be fine. At least if you really are interested." Nathaniel's eyes were born deep into mine. I was wondering what I thought and wanted. It was a yes-or-no answer, which I could give them, but I had to have more time to consider everything. As much as I wanted to be with them the entire time, five years of studying would separate me from them for this amount of time too. I was scared to lose them at that time. Of course, we would have the weekends, but what if they didn't want me anymore? If anything changed while I was hundreds of miles away, Was the thought of becoming a better relationship while we were working together all the time worth educating myself for five years and risking everything in those days of abstinence?

Chapter 11

Days passed quickly, as always. It was the first time in my life that I didn't like that. Before, I had appreciated it very much to see the seasons pass while I myself could enjoy the holidays as fast as possible over again. Now, as I have my own clinic, there are no fast-planned holidays. If I wanted, I could make them once a month. I just had to prepare everything the other week. However, I didn't want to leave it on its own. Like a newborn child, I wanted to be about it until the end of my days. Besides the fact that it would be possible since it wasn't going to run away from me some day, Addicts would exist as long as our society did, at least with the traditions we had.

"We skipped already last week; can't we make it this week either?" Lusie asked, referring to the BDSM meetings. I did not have a problem being there, but neither did I see the purpose of it. We had already found our constellation and with whom we wanted to be. Why should we meet others to talk about it?

"What about making a beautiful evening together? Just the three of us?" I tried to make the thought of that more suitable for her. May she figure out by herself what I meant. Nathaniel had already understood it before I had finished my sentence.

"What was it about the pushing?" He raised an eyebrow while he had a relaxed half smile on his normally expressionless face. Maybe not expressionless, just not readable. Like you saw, there is something, but it's hiding from you.

"What about making a story evening? Games or anything else together." Lusie named her idea, and I was at once regretting not having accepted her wish to get to the BDSM meeting. I hated creating stories. I didn't see the point of it. There are many good books, movies, and other kinds of storytellers existing; why create your own?

"Actually, that's not a bad idea. It would get us closer to one another, don't you agree, Deen?" I felt that he did it to tease me. He didn't like to tell stories himself since they could get very personal very fast. However, since he knew my thoughts about that too, he would of course like to challenge me since I declined his first wish already.

"Of course. I will listen," I decided at once, and Lusie started to laugh while she told me that this was not how it functioned. I knew that. However, I had learned in the past few months to create my own rules. Why not change all of them and create a new game altogether?

"You start." Both of them looked at me while we sat on the double bed. They were leaning against the wall, while I had to sit cross-legged, or else I would fall over.

"About what?" I said, and Lusie laughed, while Nathaniel smiled, amused. Of course, he liked me being out of control and having ideas. He had always preferred to be in charge of everything. The theme of the game was to create a story about whatever you liked, at least at the start. The others have to continue it, each with one minute of speaking. The timer was on. I had to start. Now. I would win this. In the end, even if I didn't like it, I knew I was good at it.

"In a world of leather, chains, and lace, there lived a switch, seeking his place. By day, he'd command, all bold and strong, but by night, there was a different rhythm to his song.

In secret chambers, where shadows play, He'd shed his armour and let inhibitions sway. His fantasies, submissive and sweet, In the arms of another, he'd find his retreat.

Bound and tied in silk restraints, his desires were unleashed; there was no need for restraints. With whispered commands and a gentle touch, he'd surrender willingly, his heart clutching.

His fantasies are a dance of power and grace, a delicate balance in a forbidden space. In submission, he found release. A sanctuary where his soul found peace.

So, in the quiet of the night's embrace, he'd embrace his fantasies without a trace. For in the realm of BDSM's domain, he found fulfilment, free from m disdain." Lusie had leaned back, relaxed, to listen to each of my words. Maybe even finding herself in it. However, as soon as I was finished, it was her turn to continue it. Timer on.

"In another corner, a woman awaits. Her desires are darker, shrouded in debates. In the depths of her being, a longing so deep, for a fantasy twisted, she secretly keeps.

In the role of a victim, she finds her release in the arms of a partner who honours her peace. With whispered save words and a tender caress, she explores the shadows, her heart to confess.

In the dance of dominance, she finds her surrender. In the hands of a lover, she is so careful and tender. Rapeplay, a taboo she dares to explore, with trust as the anchor, she asks for more.

For in the depths of her darkest desire, she finds liberation, her spirit on fire. In the safety of the scene, she can let go, and in the aftermath, her strength will grow.

So she walks the line between pleasure and pain in the world of BDSM, where fantasies reign. In the depths of her soul's hidden crease, she finds solace in her unique release. "I had to nod in complimenting her rhyme. I had never heard her poetry before and was almost impressed by it. Otherwise, Nathaniel, who smiled easily, was relaxed as ever. Not surprisingly, but like he had expected her to be as good as well. Now it was his turn. The last of my games started. It wouldn't be easy for him since we were all there until now. However, he didn't let anyone win. Ever. Timer on.

"And yet in the shadows, another figure stands tall, dom with a presence, commanding over all. With leather cuffs and ropes so tight, he binds his partner in the depths of the night.

With every knot and promise made, to honour her trust, never to degrade. In the art of bondage, he finds his art. Crafting a masterpiece with every part.

He guides her journey with a steady hand. Leading her through the unknown land. With each command, he sees her bloom, in the sanctuary of their private room.

For him, it's not about power or control, but nurturing her spirit makes her whole. In the dance of dominance, they find their dance. A symphony of pleasure, a sweet romance.

For in the beauty of their shared embrace. They find freedom in every trace. Bound together in love's sweet bond,

In the world of BDSM, where they both belong," I rolled my eyes at once he was finished.

"You excluded me," I pinpointed, while both of them started to laugh at me. Yes, I was in the beginning sure to win the round, but no, I wouldn't give up for now.

"Revenge," I said before we even decided which one of us wanted the round, maybe too early since I already made it clear to myself that I didn't have a chance to be it myself.

"Are you that offended by not being the best, little brother?" His words made me laugh too. I wasn't offended; it was just not what I had expected. Who could know that we were that good at the same topic?

"You know, then you asked me about where I saw myself in five years." I looked at Lusie, and she nodded with a light smile while both of them looked at me.

"If you had asked me the same for a year, I would surely have said an artist. Unrealistically, as I was. It had been a dream to stand on the stage; however, now I kind of realise that I never am going to be able to do that." I looked down at my hands while I said the last part of it. Even though I had given up on the dream, I hadn't said it out loud before. Now, it sank into me that I was ageing. Or maybe it was the clinic? I didn't want to grow old already. I wasn't even thirty yet.

"Who said that?" Nathaniel looked at me with almost a disappointed look, which surprised me. He knew my age, chances, and qualifications. Why wouldn't he be as realistic as always? There was no way I was getting on a stage any day to sing; without that, at least half the public would run away.

"Would you ever have thought about starting a private clinic on your own a year ago?" No was the answer, but was that the same? As an artist, you had to get popular, and with the clinic, I just had to find patients. Nothing else. Additionally, although I had gotten a lot of help from both of them, on stage, there would be just me. Singing wrong would be my mistake, nobody else's.

Chapter 13

As I step in front of the bed, my heart quickens with excitement and a touch of nervousness. Nathaniel stood before me, his presence both intimidating and alluring. Beside me is Deen, captivating as a switch, whose energy radiates confidence and mischief. I wondered which side he would take this time. Before, it had almost always been the submissive one.

Nathaniel's voice cuts through the silence, firm and commanding. "Take off your clothing," he commands, his tone brooking no argument. I obey without hesitation, peeling away my clothes with trembling hands. Each article of clothing discarded feels like shedding a layer of inhibition, leaving me exposed and vulnerable before them. Deen obeyed at once too. It felt a little rare to see him in the same position as I was. Both suit me, but they are also a little unusual.

Once naked, I stand before Nathaniel, his eyes devouring every inch of my skin. I feel a flush of heat rise to my cheeks as I meet their gaze, a mixture of desire and apprehension swirling within me.

With a flick of his wrist, Nathaniel produces a blindfold, and my breath catches in my throat as he secures it over my eyes. Darkness envelops me, heightening my senses and leaving me acutely aware of every sound and touch.

Deen's voice, low and seductive, breaks through the silence. "Relax, Lusie," he murmurs, his hand gently stroking my hair. "You're safe with us." I heard him say it in such a low whisper that I dwelled upon the fact that Nathaniel had noticed it. I nodded slowly, while the thought that he cared about me suited me well. Even if he showed his emotion, in the beginning I had wondered if it was just about the sex for him or if he had other feelings about it too. He wouldn't show any realness back then. However, after a while, I recognised them. Still, I wondered if I had seen them because I had been searching for them. I skipped that thought for now.

"Touch her at the breasts," as short as his command was, and large the pleasure laying behind it. At once, I heard Deen react, blindfolded. His hands searched carefully for my body. Once he had found me, we would twist in the places he needed to make me react even more intensely than in the coloured world. My body is relaxing under Deen's soothing touch. Despite the darkness, I feel a sense of trust and surrender wash over me, knowing that Nathaniel and Deen are in control; even if he too didn't see anything, my rang was still under him.

Like this, he continued for a while, until Nathaniel broke in. With whatever he had in his hands, he sent me shivers that went deep under my skin. Even though I knew that he wouldn't harm me, my mind played games with me. It knew very well how gentle the most painful image in your mind at one time could be. Roughness was, at least, honest. Creating even more pleasure inside me than anything else I had done with Deen before. It seemed to me like he was a professional. Like he had been training himself anywhere. How else could he have gotten that good at playing with me like that without even touching me once?

Nathaniel broke the silence, his voice like velvet wrapped in steel. "Kneel," he commands, and I sink to the floor without hesitation, my knees pressing into the soft carpet beneath me. Deen follows suit, mirroring my position beside me.

Nathaniel's hands roam over my exposed skin, his touch both gentle and possessive. He trails his fingers along the curve of my spine, sending shivers of pleasure coursing through me. I let out a soft moan, unable to suppress the rising tide of arousal building within me.

Deen's touch joins Nathaniel's, his hands exploring my body with a sense of curiosity and wonder. Together, they map out every curve and contour, leaving no inch of skin untouched.

As their hands roam over me, I feel a sense of liberation wash over me, as if I'm shedding the constraints of my everyday life and embracing my true desires. With each caress, I feel myself sinking deeper into subspace, a place where pleasure and pain blur into one. The fact that Nathaniel didn't ignore his own reactions suited me. Let me relax more and not watch him the entire time.

His voice, low and commanding, pierces through the darkness. "Stand," he orders, and I obey without hesitation, rising to my feet with newfound purpose.

With a firm grip, Nathaniel guides me to the other side of the room, securing my wrists and ankles with leather cuffs. I feel a thrill of anticipation course through me as I surrender to his control, my body trembling with excitement.

Deen's voice echoes in the darkness, his words a promise of pleasure yet to come. "Trust us, Lusie," he murmurs, his breath warm against my ear. "We'll take you to heights you've never dreamed of." I smiled as he said that, not because of the feelings that lay in front of me, but because he had accepted his own. Getting to know what would bring him even more pleasure and not the need to search for it in thousands of other women He had somehow found it in our dynamic. The three of us will be one forever. Not only in the spare time, but the past few weeks also at work.

I nodded, my heart pounding in my chest as I awaited their next move. With Nathaniel and Deen at my side, I know that I'm in capable hands, ready to explore the depths of my desires without reservation.

Nathaniel's hands roam over my exposed skin, his touch igniting a firestorm of desire within me. He trails his fingers along the curve of my spine, sending shivers of pleasure coursing through me. I let out a soft moan, unable to suppress the rising tide of arousal building within me.

Deen's touch joins Nathaniel's, his hands exploring my body with a sense of reverence and awe. Together, they map out every curve and contour, leaving no inch of skin untouched.

As their hands roam over me, I feel a sense of liberation wash over me, as if I'm shedding the constraints of my everyday life and embracing my true desires. With each caress, I feel myself sinking deeper into subspace as my mind relaxes while I trust them blindly.

Nathaniel's voice, low and commanding, pierces through the darkness. "Spread your legs," he orders, and I obey without hesitation, parting my thighs to his will. I feel a rush of heat between my legs as I expose myself to his gaze, my body trembling with anticipation. Shortly, I wondered if he was alright with it. Was Deen able to see him again? Images from the last time ran through my head before they were gone. At once, he continued.

With a firm grip, Nathaniel guides me to the bed, positioning me over its gentle surface. I feel the cool of it against my skin as he secures my wrists and ankles with leather restraints, rendering me completely immobile.

Deen's voice echoes in the darkness, his words a promise of pleasure yet to come. "You're so beautiful like this, Lusie," he murmurs, his breath warm against my ear. "Completely at our mercy."

I moan softly in response, my body thrumming with desire as I await their next move. With Nathaniel and Deen at my side, I know that I'm in capable hands, ready to surrender to whatever pleasures they have in store.

Nathaniel's hand comes down with a sharp crack against my exposed flesh, sending a jolt of pain and pleasure coursing through me. I cry out in ecstasy, my body arching against the restraints as I surrender to the exquisite sensation.

Deen's touch joins Nathaniel's, his fingers tracing patterns of arousal over my heated skin. Together, they administer a symphony of sensation, alternating between pleasure and pain with expert precision.

As the intensity builds, I feel myself teetering on the edge of oblivion, my senses overwhelmed by the onslaught of sensation. With each strike, I feel myself unravelling, lost in a sea of pleasure and surrender.

Nathaniel's voice cuts through the haze of sensation, his words a lifeline in the darkness. "Come for us, Lusie," he commands, and I obey without hesitation, my body convulsing with the force of my release.

As I spiral into ecstasy, I feel a sense of freedom wash over me, as if I'm shedding the constraints of my everyday life and embracing my true desires. With Nathaniel and Deen by my side, I know that I'm in capable hands, ready to explore the depths of my pleasure without reservation. As long as he wouldn't cross his own borders, that would remain the best event I would ever feel. Of course I didn't want him to do it now, but deep inside me, I wondered if it would change anytime. If he would change in any way, There was one side of me that didn't want him to do that. However, the other was ready for more and longed for it; he was ready to realise that nothing would harm him here anymore. It lay in his past, too deep to be ignored. I understood that and had some of the triggers myself. I was almost cursing myself for wanting him to forget, while I wasn't able to do it myself. Even if I hadn't experienced anything as cruel as he had.

Chapter 14

As I watch Lusie surrender to Nathaniel's commands, a surge of desire courses through me, igniting a firestorm of longing deep inside me. Every moan that escapes her lips and every tremble of her body sends a jolt of pleasure straight to my soul. I smiled at her, while another orgasm made her scream, tremble, and moan. She sounded beautiful, like she looked. Our angel she is. I would never set her free again. Nathaniel is surely not either. We have one. Nothing could destroy that. Ever.

For so long, I had hidden my desires behind a facade of indifference, afraid to embrace the depths of my own longing. As I stand here right now, I know that I can no longer deny the truth that burns within me. I didn't want to either. I had learned to accept it. Now, I almost wonder why I hadn't done that earlier. Nobody seemed to be interested in our sexual lives. We could do whatever we liked inside the safe walls of the garage, and nobody would care. People there are selfish, as I had known, but they are also almost in need of chatter about anybody. At least whose I had gotten to know.

Watching Nathaniel take control over the two of us, his dominance unwavering and absolute, awakens something primal within me—a hunger that demands to be sated. I've always been drawn to the power dynamics of BDSM—the thrill of surrendering control and exploring the depths of pleasure and pain. But until now, I had just gotten rid of the second submissive in the dynamic. However, I liked it as he gave me the chance to embrace my other, dominant side too. It was otherwise. Another type of pleasure. As a submissive, you came into another space in your mind. It would almost stop you from overthinking anything while you just waited for the orders. That was, of course, otherwise as a dom. However, I would not say that the intensity was less. Maybe comparable, just in another way, the same for me. I liked myself on both sides. The only thing I didn't like about being a judge was the constant decision-making involved. You are not finished after a session.

As Nathaniel delivered another sharp strike against Lusie's exposed flesh, I felt a surge of arousal coursing through me, my own desires rising to the surface with a newfound intensity. I ache to join them, to experience the exquisite pleasure of surrendering to Nathaniel's command, to lose myself in the intoxicating ecstasy of submission. The dominant side would belong to him. For now. If I played with Lusie alone, I would overtake her. Not that I didn't like it, but with two dominants, you had two different minds, which could make it hard to find a solution about how you want everything to be alike.

With trembling hands, I stepped forward, my heart pounding in my chest, as I approached Nathaniel and Lusie. His gaze meets mine, dark and smouldering with desire. At once, I felt a shiver of anticipation race down my spine. Without a word, he gestures for me to join them, now as the submissive part beside Lusie again. His silent command echoed in the air and threw my heart. I smiled for a second, knowing that this was all I wanted right now. No thinking.

No dwellings. No power. Just being his in every way, while he could do to me whatever he wanted. In every way he wanted. As long as he wanted. While I would obey and follow each order like I was supposed to as a sub.

With a sense of reverence, I kneeled down beside Lusie, my eyes never leaving Nathaniel's as I submitted to his will. In this moment, I feel a sense of liberation unlike anything I've ever known—a freedom born from the surrender of my own desires. Here, I wanted to stay. Not literary, but at least making it to a large part of my free time. Never had I felt so much pleasure in such a short period of time. With Jake's girlfriend, Ceceilia, there had been a lot of desire too, but in another way. I couldn't fully relax since I didn't know her or her purpose for wanting to dominate me. It also took me a bit out of the blue. Everything there took me out of the blue, which made me lock my welcome door. I was getting negative about everything I saw. Even if it was my own desire I was referring to, in that second I thought that they had manipulated me, even if I knew that my Google search would prove that wrong. Still, I wondered how he had figured that out, but not now. Maybe tomorrow or in the next few days, I could continue with the wonder. Now, I was here, safe, loved, captured in desire and lust, and lost in the thrill of BDSM. What more could a man wish for? Nothing came to my mind.

Nathaniel's hand finds its way to my hair, his touch gentle yet commanding as he guides me closer to Lusie's trembling form. With a whispered command, he instructs me to caress her skin and explore every curve and contour with a sense of reverence and awe.

As I followed his guidance, I felt a sense of purpose wash over me. As if I've finally found my true calling. Not meaning that there was nothing else that mattered in life, but right now in my private life, only the two of them are of any importance. I am a person who is not at all good in deep friendships and relationships. I could say to a person that I love her, and the other day I don't know who she is anymore. Even if the last time I had done that was long ago, it had still been me. Saying to anybody that nobody ever touched me or moved like she did, even if she was the worst of them all, came out as a usual compliment. It was the fact that we both should get anything out of it. As long as I had anybody to release my desire and lust into, she would get better self-worth. I figured it out quickly that this was something many of the girls struggled with. Staring with easy questions such as *"Do you think that I look good?" "Can I wear this tomorrow?"* or *"I know that I am not the most beautiful person?"* whatever it was, they said it for catching a compliment. For becoming more confident about themselves.

With each stroke of my hand, I feel a connection forming between us, a bond that transcends the physical and reaches into the depths of our souls. Even if it had been deep before too, I felt it burning into my skin now. Into my soul, like there was nothing that stopped it. With every breath I took and every single beat of my heart, it came deeper and deeper. Started to overtake the middle of my body. Spreading itself out to every other place, while I didn't move or speak. The only sound you heard right now was the desire in our moaning, while sometimes a hard command would be spoken. Else just my heavy breathing and harder beats of my heart, with each passing second increasing.

Lusie's breath comes in ragged gasps as I trace patterns of arousal over her heated skin, her body arching instinctively into my touch. With each caress, I feel a sense of power and control coursing through me—a heady rush that leaves me intoxicated with desire. Not a thousand women could have given me the desire I have right now. Indescribable. Good. Satisfying. The first time, I felt that I had everything I wanted, even if I neither had penetrative sex nor came until now. It would, of course, still be good, but right now I felt that our power dynamic was more than enough for my brain to take in. Both intense and illuminating, they surrounded me like I was tinier than a corn kernel. Let me give my control away, like I never wanted to have it. Surrounding my heart in a soft shadow, I couldn't pit point right now. However, I knew it felt good. Everything that felt alike could stay. Forever.

As Nathaniel continued to administer his exquisite torment, I found myself drawn deeper into the embrace of our shared desire. With every strike and every whispered command, I feel myself surrendering more fully to the ecstasy of the moment, lost in a sea of pleasure and sensation. Lost in the dynamic of our game of desire. Never wanting to leave or have anything else than this. Why had I never tried that before? Why was I so blind and uptaken by what anybody could think about me when nobody cared about what I was feeling or doing? Safe, sane, and consensual. Legal too, even if it wouldn't look like that sometimes. I had been reading so much about it and was almost a BDSM-nerd, despite the fact that I thought about it as "understanding rare ideas," never accepting that it was my own. With each word, the pleasure of desire had been building up in me, but I would ignore it. Pause for a while to burry it away with vanilla sex.

Vanilla, I regretted it. I would maybe have needed one intense session a week; instead, I chose several women a day. Never getting really satisfied. Imagine you're craving a particular type of dessert, let's say a rich, decadent chocolate cake. You've been thinking about it all day, imagining the taste of the moist cake and the creamy chocolate frosting. Finally, you go to one of the best-known bakeries and order a slice of their famous chocolate cake. As you take your first bite, you're filled with anticipation and excitement, expecting it to satisfy your craving completely. However, as good as the cake is, it somehow falls short of your expectations. Maybe it's not as moist as you hoped, or the chocolate flavour isn't as intense as you imagined. Despite enjoying the cake, you can't shake the feeling of slight disappointment, like something was missing. Still, you go each day to that bakery, only to be disappointed over and over again. Now, they showed me where the cake I searched for was. It had always been right in front of me; however, I went to the most popular instead of seeing what I wanted for myself.

And as I watched Lusie surrender to the sweet agony of Nathaniel's touch, I realised with startling clarity that this is where I belong. In the arms of Nathaniel and Lusie, I've found a sense of belonging that I've spent a lifetime searching for—a connection that transcends the physical and reaches into the depths of my soul. It had been on my mind for a long time, but finally I felt that I found it. A home. Not a place, but two people that I wanted to have by my side. Which makes me feel better. I want to make something out of the nothing I was. Which never gave up on me. I had been so blind. They have been here for several years, Nathaniel, as long as I could imagine. However, I always saw everything he had as something I would never reach. Even if I longed for it, I gave somehow up while I just had to stretch myself a little further out of my comfort zone to be almost beside him.

The reason I hadn't seen that was because I saw him running every day. Long away from me, then checking if I was fine, before he continued his marathon. Never being satisfied, while everybody praised him for all he had done. I had made a mistake this time and decided that he was selfish and greedy. Why would he turn around that often to see if I was fine then? What made me ignore this fact? He had been smart enough to please my parents while he achieved what he wanted. While I went to the left, he went to the right side. While I buried myself in everyone, while he just buried himself in work, While I was never satisfied at all but still could sleep peacefully, he wasn't satisfied either but worked each night, knowing that peaceful sleep wasn't existing for him anyway. While I rested in front of the TV, he would start to run his own clinic. As we now crossed paths again, it was me who started to run. He had tried to find the right way for years, and now he showed me it all at once. I had it so much easier than he had several years ago. He got a map and had to draw it himself on the way to start up his clinic. Yet I had thought it was him who was selfish. as blind as I was. Unaccepting as I was. as lazy as I was. That had changed. I was another man now.

Accepting me the way I wanted to be, not the way I was born. I am working hard to achieve everything I would like to have in the future—not just my job but also in my free time now with both of them. It has always been close, but sometimes it is the thing that stands right in front of us and that we don't see.

With a sense of reverence, I lean forward to press my lips against Lusie's skin, trailing kisses along her trembling flesh as I lose myself in the exquisite pleasure of the moment. And as Nathaniel's voice fills the air with whispered commands, I surrender completely to the ecstasy of our shared desire, knowing that I've finally found my true home. The place I always searched for. Beside Lusie and Nathaniel, While my heart was beating the same beat as theirs, While we suffered for the same deaths in the past, which still would affect what we would do with our future, However, beatings, deaths, and suffering are gone. For the rest of my life, I had to make amends for the mistakes I had made. Still, that was better than ever before. I felt better than ever before. This was me, the person I always wanted to be, with all its desires and achievements, making me whole and my heart complete.

"Let them judge you;
they will stop at once they see that
you don't react."

Part 2

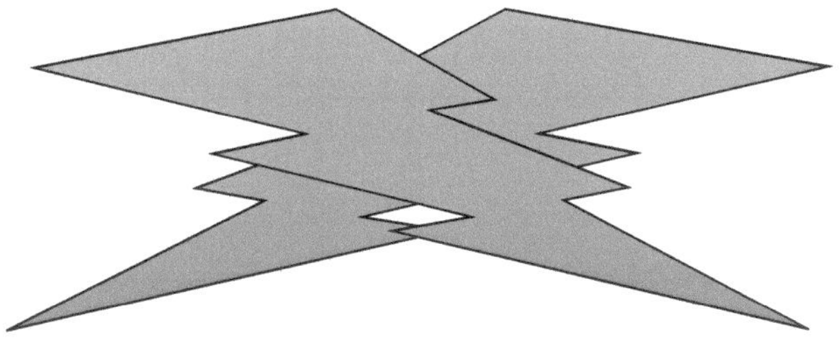

Chapter 1

"Congratulations!" Nathaniel calmly went towards me, and my smile increased with each passing second.

"Thank you so much for coming." I ran towards him and hugged him instinctively out of pleasure. That was what I had been most scared of losing—him and Deen, of course, but I had started to count them as one anyway.

It had been five years since we saw each other for the last time. I had always understood that our relationship could not, and should not, endure indefinitely like our past lives. It's not that I didn't enjoy it, but I was beginning to worry that I might grow bored with everything one day and that my overthinking could lead to negative consequences. While I was studying medicine, there was almost no time to think about anything else at all. Nathaniel did not want me to spend these years at any kind of facility, so I had to go to the best universities in the country. He and Deen had completed their doctorates at the same universities. I wouldn't have any problem with that at all.

"Where are we heading now?" I asked, challenging him with a wide smile. He wrapped his arm around my shoulders and began to walk with me toward his familiar car.

"What about getting to the restaurant there? Maybe somebody will be waiting for us?" His indirectness was failing; could he have changed too? Or was I just getting better at understanding each of his words clearly?

Years could separate us and bring us closer together. There was a large gap between their events, but I hoped that everything would turn out well again. Now that I've departed from the building where our final graduation took place, I must refrain from overthinking. A part of life ended while another began.

"I would like that," I continued to smile, but perhaps I had been stiffening a little because he always understood exactly what I was thinking and answered all of my unasked questions; without that, I would have to take further action.

"We are going to be fine. Trust me. Deen has not changed, aside from the fact that he has grown to be able to work while also having free time. Regarding myself, I am pleased that I can now resume my work. Did you read the last newsletter?" He inquired as I began to feel more at ease, his angelic voice making my heart race.

"Best statistics in the country, yes, a way to go, Mr. Perfect," he smiled honestly, maybe a little proudly. That had always been his passion. Even if he had been on top of the lists with his former clinic before, this was more like a final thing. This was a moment that held the potential to endure indefinitely.

"I hope you have had enough time to think through how you are going to make the best out of your idea." I laughed and nodded.

Indeed, five years are sufficient to educate and specialize me in a doctoral field. Even though I already had a deep understanding of both themes, which significantly shaped who I am today, They made me into who I am today, both directly and indirectly.

"We can talk about all that later; now we will just have a good time together. Fine?" I turned towards him. I made him stop. He looked down into my eyes while I was smiling like the sun itself. Perhaps Alice's smile, which Deen had described as the joy of life itself, was even more convincing.

"I missed you," I said honestly, accepting of my feelings, and years of loneliness fell on my shoulders. We had seen each other. They had visited me, but it had not been the same. I had been away, most apparently. They had been together for the first years, living in the garage, and now they have their own house anywhere beside the clinic. I had never been there before, because we would not go home on weekends or holidays. Nathaniel was very certain that I learned as much as possible—certainly more than I ever would need—about my new job. Instead of relieving symptoms, being a doctor saves lives and makes people healthier.

"You didn't want us to bring you home each weekend," he said, and I nodded with a tight smile. Yes, that was my fault, but not because I did not want to see them. It was simply because I was afraid of returning to college after graduation. I had to use these years fully to achieve as much knowledge as they had. Still, I was almost sure that Nathaniel knew more than me. Even if I had read all his books, Nathaniel would have gained a deeper understanding of his daily emotions. For him, it was not a job; it was a living reason and passion.

I turned around one last time to wave my friends goodbye. in total. Furthermore, I didn't have the time to attend college. On the other hand, I had always preferred deeper relationships to a more superficial view of people. I wondered if the end of that chapter of my life also meant that I would never see them again. That had happened the other time, too. People departed on their journey through life.

"Is Deen getting grey hair already?" I asked as we sat in his car, and he laughed. "It is not that long ago since you saw him the last time." That was partly true, since time was a relative thing. Think about the existence of the universe; I saw Deen yesterday. From the perspective of a mayfly, it was centuries ago. We humans would describe it as a half-year.

"It is summer now. We last saw each other during the winter break when we took a flight to the Maldives, but we were only there for two days due to an incident involving one of his patients. I explained to him that I had no idea how quickly time had passed. For me, it could have been a week ago, but internally, I knew that there had been too much for just a week.

"Yes, he had forgotten to inform his favourite nurse that they should only call if someone is near death, not just if they haven't urinated for a day." He rolled his eyes, and I chuckled at the typical Deen behaviour. Forgetting was a common event that often led to our separation. Half a year ago, I decided to organize a spa weekend for just Nathaniel and myself. That had been great too, even if it would have been even better with Deen's amusing statements, which he never gave up on. Luckily.

The first restaurant I visited, the Noble Five-Start China Restaurant, may have been the one with which I had the closest relationship. I recalled the first time I visited him there, shortly after his surgery, when he was in a wheelchair and everything was in order. Still, it was one of the most intense events I have in mind. It marked the beginning of our potentially unending bond. At least in the context of a human life, it was significant.

We entered, and he was the first person I saw. Deen. My smile broadened to such an extent that I felt a sense of unease, almost to the point of fear. However, we rushed towards each other, disregarding the fact that we were in a prestigious restaurant, which was expected to be quiet and provide more formal service.

"Deen," I said as he uttered my name aloud, and we found ourselves there, barely able to hold each other. The longing for the other person, who was a part of our own, was deeply felt. We have belonged together for many years. Yet it had been a long journey of accepting and creating such a "perfect" relationship with the three of us. There were no longer any singles or duos, just the three of us together. That was how I imagined the most beautiful time for the rest of my life.

"I love you," he whispered into my ear, while we were still standing in the middle of the restaurants, our arms around each other. Maybe our bonding was so strong that no one here dared to leave us. At least it felt like we needed this moment for the two of us; too long had passed since we saw each other the last time, more than just a few days. Still, feelings remained like longing, desire, and wishing for a happy life together. Dwellings that this wouldn't happen had disappeared from my side again. It had always been part of what I had been most frightened that it could happen; beside that, any of them has an incident, and... Don't think about that now. We are alive. We were happy together again. The trio, destined to last forever, hoped to do the same. I was ready, and it appeared to me that they were there too. We didn't have to count days anymore; we could start counting the years in which we would see each other every single day. We were healthy, still young, and most importantly, designed for each other.

Chapter 2

"Sorry for that, I am late." Deen entered the restaurant, as I had already been sitting there with Nathaniel for about half an hour, waiting for him and food to come.

"Come here, Lusie." I stood up and went to him, and he smiled almost as happily as I did. That was seldom the case. Even if he didn't hesitate to show his emotions, who could top my smile?

"Or wait a moment." He stretched out his hand, symbolizing me to stop. "Turn around once." I did what he wanted with the same smile as earlier, which surely made the sun a concurrence.

"How did you do that? I rolled my eyes and walked towards him, giving the charmer a hug. It was both sweet and cheesy; however, that was Deen. Deen was the person I had been missing for years, someone I looked forward to seeing every single day. Humorous, easy to talk to and laugh with, while also being kind of sexy.

"You didn't get any worse either; you started training?" I asked as he sat down. Was that question funny? It had to be an insider, because before any of them answered, they both would laugh out loudly. Not at me, but heartily, like it was anything they had been talking about earlier.

"Explain the insider; let me laugh about that too," I demanded, while they both calmed themselves down again. Nathaniel didn't express his emotions in a consistent manner. To laugh out loud meant to him that he smiled for longer than just a hint of a second before getting the normally neutral gaze again.

"Let me explain it," he said to his younger brother, who tried to start anywhere before he commanded him to stay silent.

"There was that patient, a boy in his late thirties. He was in Deen's department at the clinic and had his last weak with a girl." This was their new system, which they had told me about before. Each Friday, they had a cosy evening for the entire clinic. Yes, both cancer and withdrawal patients. On that day, they would get on the stage with all the newcomers, and whose last weak was there. Since it was always around the same count of people, whoever would leave would get a newcomer to introduce them to the routines of the clinic. Most often, they would belong to the same department, but sometimes they would be mixed too. The idea with that was that each person tell their stories and explain not only the daily routine but also how well the treatment functions there. For the cancer patients, they are fine after the months of diet, MRI's, the operation, and training outside. For the withdrawal patients, could this be the cold turkey, which they usually started with, and afterwards the free-time activities, psychological help, and support they get to find another place to come home to, or a stable mindset, which makes them clearly avoid anything that could possibly harm them in the future?

"While the man looked like he at least spent five hours in the gym a day, Deen looked beside him like spaghetti," Nathaniel said flatly, without showing any sense of affection, while Deen shook his head and laughed about the event that surely had happened afterwards.

"His companion would be from my department and in her late fifties. However, it didn't take a long time before they chattered like they were the best friends." I imagined them and already laughed at the constellation.

"He would sit beside her bed all day, and for those who didn't know them, it felt like he was her son, instead of a stranger she had gotten to know less than a week ago," he explained while Deen pushed him to get to the point even faster, and I already had some idea of what might have happened, which let Deen start going to the gym sometimes.

"On his last Friday, he would get on stage with the woman and perform a song about how much he liked his doctor, but he was always scared that the next gust of wind would blow him away. The woman sang in her second voice. It sounded really good, and they got the entire clinic to laugh about that for the entire time she spent there," he explained, and I laughed at the creativity only by his telling.

"Before he left that night, we would say that I had to start to train if I wanted that he wouldn't return and continue the ballade." I shook my head at their rare private joke, while I could see now why they laughed. On the other hand, it showed me that I had been away for a long time. That was just one story, and it did not last very long; aside from that, the women had already left the clinic by now. However, it was not only this that I had been missing. My studies had included that I got apart of another environment, which did fit me well for the time. Yet, I had been thinking about home, the brother, every single day and was looking forward all the time to coming back. Here I was. I was still wondering if it would ever get like it had been, or if we had changed too much.

"Tell us now a little about your plans. At least me. I know that my dear brother has started to change the western department already, but I still do not know what you want to do there. He always said, "You have to tell me everything yourself, since he surely wouldn't get to explain it in the euphoric way you would." Deen told me this while rolling his eyes at his brother's hesitation. I laughed for a moment before I got myself together and started to tell my exact plan.

"I don't want to start anything completely new for the clinic. We are going to remain for withdrawal and cancer; I just have specialized myself in child and teenager treatment," I explained, and his eyes widened in shock.

"That is not going to end silently," he said before I could finish my plans, judging them already like a typical Deen thing to do. Never listening, always having set up an opinion about anything he knew nothing about.

"At first, you do have young patients too," he cut off before I could say another word. "Yes, but not children or teenagers." They are grownups, at least in our age or older," he defended his opinion, and I took a deep breath while the waiter arrived with our food. We thanked her kindly, but she came as fast back to our discussion as we had stopped with it before she came.

"The afterthought," I began, but before I could get to the third word, Deen argued more intensely. "You do need a complete set-up; yes, the idea can be beautiful and heartwarming, but still, you are treating children. There are parents." Now it was me who cut him off, just continuing his impoliteness. "Thank you, Deen, but I am not a fool. I know that most of the kids who will be there will hopefully have parents and maybe even struggle at home. The most problematic event with that might be that their legal guardian will not send them to us." He tried to cut me off again, but this time Nathaniel would help me out. "Deen, if that is too personal and heartbreaking for you, Say it. This is not only unprofessional but also impolite. One more time, and I cut your budget," he threatened, and Deen leaned back while raising his hands in forgiveness.

"To begin at a start anywhere; I know that it might not be easy, but we are trying to finance my department just from donations, a small percentage from state support funds for drug prevention, and the rest from your departments." Now he stood up and made the entire restaurant look at us as he pointed out that "you are not going to get a cent of support from my department. It is not like I do have it easy to get patients who are able to pay the costs of the treatment." He was obviously offended, but the cool, calm voice from Nathaniel cut still more through the room as he just said, whose three words with an indescribable power over his brother "Sit down. Now" It didn't take Deen more than a second to sit beside us again and excuse the coincidence with the rest of the restaurant, while I sat there in shock, getting smaller out of shame for each single second that continued. What made him that negative about the new department? It is not like he was going to change anything; they already had finished the renovation by next week, and the first patients would arrive on Friday of the same week too. It was me who got thrown into the cold water and was supposed to scream, not him. However, could Nathaniel be right in saying that the theme of having young patients at the clinic didn't bother him but touched him personally? Could it be possible that he saw himself in them too much and was scared to show too many emotions while having to be a professional doctor? I really wondered if that might be the case, and somehow I hoped that it wouldn't be anything that couldn't change. Saving the youth was a passion that lingered inside me while I hadn't grown up myself. I did want to give them the chance, not only to have a wonderful childhood but also to stand on their own two feet as soon as they are grown up, like I had to too.

Chapter 3

The clinic was not as convenient as it once was. It was at least three times the size of Nathaniel's former one and had undergone many renovations since we started. The case had gotten us many supporters, but mainly more well-known than we once were. Marketing was not necessary anymore, at least not for Nathaniel's departure; he surely had to have at least twice the size to treat everyone he wanted. Unfortunately, it was only us. Fortunately, it was to the monopole's benefit, but it was still disheartening to realize that no one else had the courage to challenge the pharmaceutical industry. They'd rather get rich the easy way, making money while concentrating on their patients' symptoms.

"Good morning. "You look good today, Mrs. Stowell," I said as I passed one of her nurses, who had worked for me since day one. Our team had increased a lot. My department had enough space to accommodate twenty-five patients, including Nathaniels, but I needed to convince him that I only had fifteen employees, compared to his twenty-one. Sometimes, they would assist me if any of my patients fell ill, but I didn't want to rely on such a large backup plan as he had in case the influenza or another virus decimated half the building.

Altogether, I had not only gotten used to my job here, but I also really loved it. Seeing everybody each Friday was motivation to continue everything. Not only did the new arrivals always have a sparkle in their eyes as they entered the building and experienced everything for the first time, but those who left also had a distinct look in their eyes that held an unexplainable significance for me. Thankfulness. They have a purpose and a plan for carrying on with their lives. The chapter came to an end, but a new one had already begun when they stepped into the clinic on their first day. They didn't realise that they had to start over from the beginning.

"Good morning, everybody." Each morning, we started our day with a precise meeting at half nine a.m., after breakfast. For some, this was the explanation of hell—the time, not the conversations themselves; for others, this was the highlight of the day. The good mixture made it complete.
"May we begin by discussing the negative facts that some of you experienced yesterday?" In the background, there are two security guards standing. Despite their hidden presence, they remain accessible in the event of an emergency. Luckily, we never had any complications until now.

"I lost my libido," the comedian, who had been here for his third week, said. The rest of the room laughed for a moment at his directness, but I nodded while beseeching someone to continue. There was no pressure, but it was easier to talk to many strangers rather than one weird doctor, as some had been calling me. I wouldn't take it personally, but I see the progress we make each morning at our meeting.

"I saw you twice yesterday; that came to me like a shock, too." Another specialist pushed the humour up while joking about my appearance. I did not take everything seriously, and I laughed for a while before I had to assure myself that he would see everything twice.

"You can calm down. I didn't take any drugs that I used to have as a child too. Just a migraine, which makes that for a few seconds or sometimes even minutes." I frowned and noted that, since I surely would have to check this up again afterwards and give him advice for how he could treat that.

After another round, they were all there, ready for the positive events, which always went much better to talk about than the pessimistic ones, which desperately searched for any lack in our treatment that they could name at first.

"I didn't think about drinking anything the entire evening yesterday while we sat and played cards. Typically, we would always have at least one bottle of wine during our evenings with my former friends, said the banker woman, who had been here for her second week. I praised her for her progress, while another one eagerly wanted to share his progress too.

"I had the best sex of my life yesterday, also without any alcohol influence," some laughed, while others looked in shock at him. I laughed as I wondered which of the few women here had been fortunate enough to share that moment with him. Or unfortunate enough, since I would not describe him as any handsome man. The years of work on the construction site had shaped him. At least the beer had shaped him more than the muscles from the hard work.

"I wrote a song for your girlfriend, which I am going to sing as a welcome gift tomorrow." Of course, they had heard about her beginning to work next week. Still, I didn't like the thought that even more people would be here, and I could not control myself. Young addicts could cause more struggles than progress or make a positive impact on our clinic. If they were just half as foolish as I had been, I would see our clinic closed in less than half a year. It needed just one person to take its life; without that, we noticed its suicidal thoughts. Everything else, including our excellent call, would vanish instantly.

"Good, I believe we have finished our morning greeting and will see you again tomorrow." I am looking forward to hearing about your progress," I said as I was already on the way to the western department. Lusie's department. It was both next to mine and Nathaniels, almost in the middle of them, while it did not offer more space than around fourteen or fifteen patients.

"Hi Deen, I am sorry for the fact that we took you out of the blue." She started to apologize. We had not been taking anymore since the dinner. The past few nights, I have been trying to figure out what would be best to do. It wasn't a personal matter, and I appreciated her idea. However, I knew that the outcome wouldn't be favorable. I knew that. Something had been telling me this for a while now, and I was afraid of not reacting and seeing the consequences in the near future.

"We are fine, Lusie. It is just the fact that this is not only going to get complicated; as you turned it down, it is going to get impossible to be made in a safe way," I explained, and she smiled at the fact that I was not mad at her. At least she saw the positive side of it.

"If you would come with me and listen to what I have to say, you might have understood the fact that we have been taking care of every rare idea that might come to their mind," she explained while we went upstairs on the way to her part of the clinic.

The wall, floor, and even the interior have not only undergone fire protection verification but also remain unbreakable. No sharp knives or anything else that might give them the possibility of hurting themselves is available anywhere. There is nothing breakable that could potentially cause harm. Additionally, each of my employees has a wealth of pedagogical, psychological, and other experiences, and three of them are also doctors. As she explained this, my eyes widened in shock, wondering where she had been looking for her workers or if she had been printing them the way she wanted them to be.

"We are going to have at least seven occupations for each of the sicknesses at all times. We finance the treatment of cancer patients at 150%, generating a minor profit. The other way around, it goes with the withdrawal patients, since they think that the danger is too great that they will relapse," she explained sadly, and I saw for the first time how much she had been preparing herself for this over the past years. She was not like me. He was an adventurer who didn't care about his education and stood up each day to get to college. No. Not at all. She had been there every single day, I could tell. She studied at home while taking further courses in her free time. It had taken her five years to become a doctor with a passion for helping young people, and now I came and talked like a fool against all her ideas. What have I been reading and researching? The only thing I had, which she did not, was basically my own experience. There is nothing to be proud of at all.

"I am sorry. I should not have reacted like that. I have underestimated you," I explained silently while I was looking at the ground. The next time I saw her, she would lean into me and give me a welcoming, warm, and heartwarming acceptance kiss on my lips. I missed that girl. I had known her for a long time, yet I nearly forgot what it was about her that kept me waiting. Well, it was just her. In every single way. She not only had a sharp tongue, but her body, her movements, and her way of thinking, all while maintaining an innocent and angelic demeanour. Still, I knew her desires as well as she did mine. In another world, we are normal, but here, we may not be considered alike. On the other hand, who would care? We are surely not. I had learned fully to accept myself, my sexuality included. I had been a fool to take so long to do that. However, it took as much time as it needed.

In the past few years, I have spent parts of my free time volunteering on the scene. I have contributed to the preparation of parties, stood at the bar for the entire evening, or assisted with cleaning on the same evening or other days. My friends there are now all in this scene. People understood and liked me for the way I was, with all my edges and rounding's. Or was that wrong to say about a man?

"Just tell me if you need any help or advice, but I am sure that you already have an excellent plan for everything by now," I told her, as she had not pulled back but remained in a warm hug in my now muscular arms.

"Actually, I wanted to ask you if we could get out of your morning routine," she said, and my eyes widened. I had to fight hard against the initial enthusiasm of declining everything at once. I swallowed deeply and slowly started to accept the fact that she was not only always home but also a colleague of mine. Nathaniel and I had always steered the entire clinic; now we would do it as a trio, even if he surely would do the main managing like he always had done. It wasn't that she was a woman, or that I didn't consider her capable of handling this job. Just the fact that something changed in my usual environment hit me harder than it should have done with five years of preparation. Somehow, I had been thinking that she would just work as a co-doctor for either me or Nathaniel, and I never realized that she would really start her own department just by herself.

"I will think about it and talk with my patients about what they think about that tomorrow morning, okay?" I asked her, and she nodded gratefully. More than she should have. Was I such a bad person? I didn't intend to come across as so harsh yesterday. I was just not good with changes. The past few days, everything had turned out another way, and I wondered if I would appreciate it or not while I tried to get used to it.

"Good morning, everybody. Today, I have a question for you before we start." I asked them if they were interested in having

teenagers here as well, so they could learn immediately and avoid starting with these complexities later in life. I could already hear the negative response, which I had figured would come.
"Yes, that's a great idea." The entire room cheered, and I almost left in disbelief. Was it really only me that was such an egoist? I enjoyed my morning sessions with them and was delighted to hear them talk more freely. At times, there is a hint of sexuality involved. On the other hand, no children under the age of five would be here. They had surely heard worse before. Maybe it wouldn't make such a big change in the end.

The thought was mine before I realized that it was acceptance, as it was called. I was open to the idea of our clinic adopting a new structure and welcoming new, younger patients who would be just a few feet behind our walls.

It was not only me and Nathaniel anymore. Lusie is also a part of it now. On the other hand, had she not always been a part of us since we met her? Was it not just a good point that she would also be closer here, rather than a fact that I had to back out of? I loved her in every single way and eagerly hoped that she would really forgive my scepticism. It was wrong to judge a new start. Nobody had been doing that to me, either. Otherwise, I would surely have given up before I started; I was not as strong as she was.

Chapter 4

I was awake at five a.m. and almost ran furth and back—too much energy I did have. Nathaniel went downstairs with me and laughed about my enjoyment, as well as a little nervousness. It took me five years to prepare for the event, which would begin today. The first patients would arrive today. There are five for withdrawal and four for cancer. I was literary shacking. We had planned a little show tonight because we wanted them to feel truly welcome. However, there would not only be the kids but also their parents most often. At least for cancer patients, it would be very common. Before our statistics improved, they might be able to rest and care for their youngest family members without harbouring any negative feelings towards us.

"When will that start tonight?" I inquired as I moved back and forth in the kitchen, attempting to prepare our breakfast. It was the first time he was watching me while I did that, but after some hesitations, he accepted that I had to put my energy into anything right now.

"I already told you twice, after dinner at six p.m.," he explained, and I nodded at the known fact. I assured myself that there was still plenty of time, and I managed to calm down a bit, which had already made a significant difference.

During our breakfast, we created some paperwork for each of our departments, as well as for Nathaniel's entire clinic. He showed me some tips and tricks he had learned through his life. Something that I really appreciated. If I only got half as good as he was at being a perfect leader for everybody, I would be more than delighted.

"Good morning, early birds," Deen said downstairs. The new house had two floors, was similar to how Jake's home had been, since that was our inspiration. The only difference was that we also had a rustic interior. At times, I wondered who made the decision, given the practical differences. The decision was primarily based on how it appeared, as well as your perception of stepping back in time each time you entered our home. One of Nathaniel's vintage cars stood in the garage beside our house, but the rest would remain in the garage, where we once had been sleeping, for safety reasons.

"Hey, what did they say about incorporating us into your morning routine?" I asked him, and it took a second for him to understand what I meant; at least it seemed like that. For some beats, he just stood there, frozen, while looking at me intensely.

"You are welcome to be part of it. ""If you do not want to jump into the cold water from tomorrow on, you can come with me in half an hour," he explained while sitting down and dressing himself with a role and some honey.

I was really looking forward to that." He smiled for a short second as he saw my reaction before he said, "You are welcome as long as you don't bring any trouble into the group with your youth." I rolled my eyes and laughed a little more, thinking that if anyone could cause trouble, it might be me.

The difference between our withdrawal departures was mainly that the adults he had would want to come away from their addiction. Whose I had, often also just worried parents, which sent them to us. I thought the combination between them would work well. The older ones could explain to the newcomers how it worked out for them to become addicted to their everyday lives and how "cool" it really is in the end. Furthermore, I was looking forward to seeing how they reacted, which may just be a step above death and a life. That changed a point of view while you saw it, and it will have a large impact on them. I was very certain about that.

"Good morning, everybody. Today we have a newcomer, which you surely already have heard about," he nodded towards me, giving me a sign that I could start to present who I was.

"Hello everybody, my name is Lusie, and I am the guilty one who wants to track the youth to that place." Some of them laughed, while others simply listened in silence with a smile. I was almost shocked at how easy and humorous the atmosphere here was. Deen had truly reached something big here, much larger than I had expected it to be. I was truly glad that it might be a good start for my patients here every day too. Being part of that could be extremely helpful to my withdrawal patients.

"Are you his girlfriend?" somebody asked, and I looked at Deen, who did the same towards me. We both smiled for a moment, and it might be obvious. "Yes, we are together," we said, careful not to refer to ourselves as a couple to avoid inciting unwarranted gossip. Trio, not a couple. We had to be a couple in a few years, but that was something nobody was interested in thinking about. Hopefully, we had many decades until we would have to reach that unfortunate moment.

"Okay, if we show her how we usually start with the negativities from the past day," Deen led them to a start, while they all remained polite in silence. Hopefully, my teenagers will not do anything to upset that atmosphere. Changes may occur, but if the environment doesn't return to its original state, it won't guarantee our survival.

"I went to the gym yesterday morning but did not have a free mind the rest of the entire day," one of the men said, while everybody started to look at him in confusion.

"What made you feel like you would not feel relaxed like usual?" Deen inquired, but the man missed eye contact. I wondered how long he had been there, but he looked like he was not familiar with everything already.

"I missed my wife," a tear streamed from his eyes, prompting nearly half the room to rise and join him during that difficult moment. Later, Deen told me that he had started a huge business once. However, after one of his opponents killed his wife, he decided to give up everything. He became not only afraid to go out every day, but he also experienced boredom for the first time in his life, which exacerbated his suffering. In the end, he started to drink, something he had never done in his life before. It wouldn't take long until he was really addicted.

"Would you like to share your ideas of how to start a business one day with my younger patients?" After the meeting, I asked him, and his eyes lit up at finding a purpose again. "Of course, that would be wonderful," he said as he began to share his story, after which I enumerated the specific activities his company had been involved in.

Patients would help patients, that was the structure of our clinic, which not only illuminated some costs, but also showed them that they still had an story to tell. They shared their stories not just with us, but also with numerous individuals who were keenly interested. They had lived a life full of experiences and knowledge that were too significant to our society to simply pass away. Despite succumbing to drug addiction, they managed to amass a substantial amount of wealth. The only drug you get asked for why you do not take it. It is the only drug that enjoys legal status in nearly every region of our planet, and it also enjoys widespread cultural acceptance.

Later, I was busy making the last preparations. I looked at the watch the next time, at four p.m. In an hour, they would start to arrive. I was furious about not making any mistakes and checked every room at least ten times before Nathaniel finally led me downstairs. We would cooperate, but in a different way. Each week, he would receive my newly arrived cancer patients. Together, we would perform the operations, and I would assist him in the best way I could. In the end, this was meant to make the poor youth relax while they heard that even the much older patients got a new chance at life.

Downstairs, the preparations for dinner had already started, with half an hour remaining. Patients who wanted could help. That was not my duty. Still, at least five of them were their fast helpers, who came every single day before each meal and enjoyed being helpful. I was curious about the activities they would engage in during their free time. The plan was that the upcoming withdrawal patients would get someone from the adult department this week. We might change that after some weeks, while seeing the point of view of each of them. Those who are strong and proud of their recovery from addiction may have the opportunity to host a newcomer for a week. Hopefully, that would conquer the most part of them.

"Hallo, nice to meet you all. My name is Lusie, and I will be the responsible doctor for you throughout your stay. Let us start with a good meal; just follow me," I said to them, more calm than the sprint my heart was taking. Luckily, such a run would not last long; soon, I knew, I would be calmer and more relaxed. It was just a matter of time.

"Here, just take a seat. I will get the others too," I explained, while today both the parents and patients would be part of the first dinner here. Those who had been chosen for the start were all from families that cared about their children's wellbeing. Already, those who are going to come next week partly had this benefit. Today, I wanted to give myself an easier start so that they would stay with me while I tried to follow our plan as much as possible.

"Hello, my dear publicum for the evening," Deen began shortly after the meal on stage. My heart made jumps and somersaults, while my smile was similar to the sun's charisma. Everyone listened until now in silence, including my nine newcomers. Luckily.

"I will outline a brief plan for our Friday special tonight, as we will be filling an entire new department within the next few weeks." Everybody cheered at once, and my heart beat faster. That was it. The rest of the clinic responded enthusiastically. The youth are now receiving opportunities from us, eliciting joyous cheers and laughter.

"We will, as always, start with the clinic's song altogether; afterwards, volunteers can come up for their own performances. In about an hour, we plan to have the leaders from all the departments introduce themselves briefly, along with a small surprise. They all listened, while some showed their emotions in a quick laughter or with a silent smile. It spoke to how much they loved this together. There was no exact arrangement. Yet, the patients sat not only in their used departments. Some of them even made a conscious effort to interact with others, gaining insight into diverse ideas and perspectives. It was altogether more and better than illuminating.

Before I could tell that we had to start, the entire room was filled with a melody. The clinic song. Deen and Nathaniel initiated their partnership by singing the clinic song. They wanted to do it together, which meant that they also wanted their patients to have anything they shared. We are not many strangers to one another; no, not at all; we are like a community, supporting each other's wishes and beliefs. Singing together showed how common our struggles could be, even while we were standing on the other side of the globe.

"The weather is not forever,

Whatever pressure or terror we brought,.

Members of an adventure we are now on.

Whenever, wherever, and whoever

In our centre, it is a pleasure now.

The refrain everyone sang together sent shivers down my spine. The entire room was filled with that lovely, meaningful melody. After that, parts of the room stayed silent and looked to Deen and his withdrawal group, which was standing up to start their part.

We don't have to be a model,

Just come away from the bottle.

Will pass what once was normal,

Come away from the daily quarrel.

Press the throttle now with us.

After they had finished their all-too-true verse, everybody started again. I had not heard the song before, but now I could sing the refrain with them.

> The weather is not forever,
>
> Whatever pressure, terror us brought.
>
> Members of an adventure we are now.
>
> Whenever, wherever, whoever
>
> In our centre is pleasure now

Nathaniel, who had the strength of the cancer department, stood up now or sang while they were sitting their verse. I smiled while shivers ran through me endlessly as they continued the lovely clinic song.

Whatever mattered once, like a hammer it comes.

An answer of life's disasters, a new chapter had to start.

Like a sneaking panther, mastering it all.

Gather for an answer, what matters is to come away from it all.

No disaster the cancer was, we mastered it we all.

I could relate to it, as it had been the same for me. Like a sudden hammer blow, the diagnosis had hit me. It was long ago now, still I will still remember that day forever. Whoever sang the song now had exactly experienced the same in any way. All of them thought that was the final road, before they heard about the branch of the clinic, which they would decide to take.

The weather is not forever,

Whatever pressure, terror us brought.

Members of an adventure we are now.

Whenever, wherever, whoever

In our centre is pleasure now

Through sleepless nights we all survive

May took us by surprise, there where no goodbyes.

Paradise gave us other highs, alive.

Survived the deeps there the knife once strife's.

Apologize, it is to nice to be alive for us

I had to pass the new part. Tears were swelling up in my eyes as I recognised that they too had been thinking about having to say goodbye forever. I remembered the unbearable thought all too well. It still stung inside me. However, I still sang the last refrain with my full heart and voice.

The weather is not forever,

Whatever pressure, terror us brought.

Members of an adventure we are now.

Whenever, wherever, whoever

In our centre is pleasure now"

"Good to go, everybody. We are getting better each time we sing that. Now let us continue with your own creative song ideas" Deen moderated, and the first patients stood up on their way to the stage. I leaned back for the first time in years to relax while listening to the beautiful ideas they had. Even a song for me as a welcome gift. I was speechless. Unexplainable thankful. Here, I wanted to work and achieve the goals I had with the kids. They would also be able to experience such feelings one day.

Chapter 5

Since the Friday event started, I have not seen Lusie stop smiling once. She was illuminated by the evening's result. It wasn't exactly the same as every other evening, but it was comparable. Our part was mainly the new one today. Normally, Deen would be on stage for speeches and sing some songs, but more with patients than on his own. It was their evening. We would do anything similar to what we had planned today, and because of that, it is important for the children to feel safe here. They came straight from a warm, protected home to our clinic. They may have struggled or fought against anything, but this was a new place. A new start. This is particularly true for patients who have chosen to withdraw. This isn't the case for the impoverished children who were diagnosed with cancer at a young age. However, for them, we would offer a long, wonderful life.

"Okay, thank you; that was awesome. Before we embark on our usual week-partners, we would be delighted to show our own performance, which may give you a very deep look into our lives. Nathaniel, Lusie, please don't leave me alone on stage right now. Music on," he said, and it started already while we made our way onto the stage together. Usually, I do not enjoy doing it for that many people. Today, it was for a reason. I would be fine. We would be fine. It was just to reassure those who were still dwelling on that fact that everything would turn out okay.

The first verse was mine; we'd been writing the song for the past week since Lusie returned. However, it was called "United.".

"As a reaction of my past it happened.

Could write an album of that dragon.

No distractions, just a dozen actions.

Imagine me jumping over that canyon."

Lusie continued following me. The entire room was silent while they listened to every word that echoed through the show room. The light was shining on the three of us while we were united in the moment.

"The repeat of work was needed in the street.

Never believed, I had to seat after a final beat.

Treated well, learned to believe.

He was my shield, that I needed to keep."

The guitar solo would guide them from each of our verses to the next. Before the refrain started, which we would sing together, Deen would sing his verse of our unition.

"Neither am I fully green; it's also just a scene.

With fifteen drove like a limousine into the stream.

Never gleamed in a magazine, screamed more into the gasoline.

Started my dream, finally clean."

His text was not only personal for him, but also for me. I imagined each scene pictorially, as I had been seeing it like that. Yes, he used a lot of synonyms, but it was Deen. With every word, he described his past in the most correct way. He didn't mention everything, of course, but he may have highlighted the experiences that shaped him the most.

 "It was a rough start months past.

Both with new lungs, plus a month against drugs.

Came like a rush the crush,

Once together, united forever"

The echoes from the long pronunciation of the last word persisted in the building for a long time. As each of us began to sing their line, they had almost vanished.

 "I would spend the head for no dead"

As I began, images of the three deaths that had occurred at my former clinic flashed through my mind. The man with the heart attack, Lusie's mother, and, in the end, Alice, which was the curse of my biggest mistake, Abstinence. Not for a long while, but long enough to make it happen...

"Yet, we all have to take the next step."

Lusie continued, and I found myself thinking about how Deen tried to run away from it. After the common holidays at once to Dubai, we were thereafter confronted with it even worse before we could all make the next step. In that case, I would even say that we were standing right in its footprints.

"Set next to her bed; don't forget.".

It did that too, but I was thinking about what happened as I opened the door to Alica's room. It was the last time I had done that, and then she was alive. Their mouths clinched together, like an end would come soon. Longing. Desire. Lust. All that before everything broke together. Rest in peace, half-sister. You will always remain, at least in my mind. Even if I am dwelling on the fact the fact that Deen has forgotten it completely, he had not mentioned a word about her after the funeral. He had not endured a lifetime of suffering; he had moved on more quickly than one might have assumed.

Yet I see you are scared,

"It was meant to be cared for, to pass the felt to the end."

Lusie's short interlude was like the rest of the song, with several meanings. For those who listened, it was about the newcomers, but it was also about a multitude of others we had encountered.

"It was a rough start months ago.

Both with new lungs, plus a month against drugs.

It came like a rush to crush,

Once together, united forever."

We sang the refrain one last time together before cheering and applauding shaped the entire room. That was how it started. Lusie was now an official member of it all. I had been looking forward to that moment. It had never been satisfying to see her alone at home while we were at work. I always knew that there was something lingering inside her. This was particularly evident when I discovered her casually reading my medical books.

"Thank you all very much." Deen started, and the three of us remained on the stage. Now, the newcomers would be paired with their partners for the final week. Hopefully, it would turn out the way we wanted it to. On stage, he began to beg each of the nine children. I did, of course, not have four patients left in the cancer department each week. However, this time each of mine got two children "to take care of." They did not have to put much time and effort into it; they could adjust it like they wanted. On the other hand, I already saw them adopting them for a few weeks, almost as if they were their own children. One of them had breast cancer and was not older than 32. She was not able to give birth by herself anymore. As a result, we decided that she would greatly appreciate it if she had two weeks left here to guide them through the start of their illness. Another one would just be the last week here, but he has not seen his own children since he arrived here. I had been talking with him about the idea of the system long before that, and it was assured that he could help out with that too. Since the first time I mentioned it, he has been very interested in volunteering.

The five withdrawal patients got their guides from Deen's department. I did not know much about his patients. However, since they stayed around a month each, he had more arrivals and departures every single time.

At the end of the evening, Lusie spent two more hours upstairs to suit her new patients in the new environment, even if she too had further employees who could help her afterwards. Overall, we had so many workers that it would be fine to take up to two weeks off if we wanted to someday. Already now, I did have a plan for how we could use our first time off exactly.

As soon as Lusie had returned home, we would open up for some friends to come to us. It was a long day, but that was a good way for her to get to know others, not just clinic-related people at once. It was a good mix of people; Deen was close, and some I liked. All of them were there from the scene, and we had been attending several events. This was the first we had at our own place.

"Such beautiful furniture. I love that style, but my dear husband does not allow me to make everything alike it." The discussion started once they entered. "Yes, it is neither easy to clean nor practical at all," her sub said. They had been married for several years. In the bedroom, she may have been the boss, but otherwise they lived on the same eye level.

"How have your studies been? They have been telling so much about you, but always with the emphasis that you are not going to be here before today," she explained while looking at nobody else but Lusie, who was smiling broadly at the mention that we had been looking forward to her arrival. I hoped that it wouldn't shock her, since it was, in a way, what I hoped she suspected.

"It was fine, but I missed them every single day. Though I got to know many interesting new people, I am all too good at ending chapters," she explained, and I wondered if she meant that it was easy for her to say goodbye to a time that she from the start knew was primary.

They continued to talk for a while. In between those, I had prepared some snacks for all of us. Deen was busy offering people drinks. Without alcohol, of course. In that house, there had never been a drop from that source.

As late as it got, the chatter drifted from everyday life to more kinky themes. It was not the only thing they could clearly talk about. However, it was one of the common interests we all shared, making it one of the main themes of every single evening we met.

"How did your relationship work again?" Nathen, is the dom from both of you while Deen is a switch?" Sara asked. She was always one of the most curious people I knew. She did not bother with wondering if themes could be very private sometimes; she just asked. Even if it was usually in their community to talk about everything scene-related openly, without much shyness, It made it surprisingly easier for me to talk to them. I did not have to feel that I was wasting my time with hours of small talk before getting to the theme I wanted to talk about. It made me relax more and piqued my interest in the primary themes they were discussing.

"Yes, well, it's a long time ago that we did anything alike. However, Deen used to switch while I was the submissive and Nathaniel the dominant." Lusie was a little unsure, so she looked further in between us. She was right. The last time we saw us, sex had not been a huge priority. Since we generally maintained an open relationship, I observed that Deen occasionally had contact with both men and women, but not often, as we both spent most of our time at the clinic. For me, it was the same anyway. I enjoyed our sessions, but it wasn't needed for a happy life for me. It delighted me more to know that both of them were healthy and okay.

"Borring, you will have to move on again," she challenged Lusie, causing her to become slightly uncomfortable. However, Sara gently placed her hand on her shoulder and reassured her, saying, "Relax; I am just kidding. I had some fun with Deeny while you were away. However, while I am also a switcher, my primary role is submissive. Therefore, it did not hold that long before I was searching for another one." In that moment, Deen glanced at them and remarked, "Yes, she didn't tolerate me more than twice either." He said this with ease, showing no signs of intimidation when discussing such sensitive topics. Like that, it was usually here. If I did not have any specific questions, I would most likely remain listening. In the end, I liked them as friends but was not interested in having any sessions since, for me anyway, there was nothing sexually penetrative. At least I thought, too, that nobody was interested in what I wanted to have. I didn't bother to search, since, as I said, it was just sex, nothing I needed.

Suddenly, my phone vibrated. A call. I took it at once. That was the benefit of living close to the clinic. I did not have to stay there, but she was always available. At present, I had to depart from them for the night.

Chapter 6

"I'll have to go now," we said, looking each other deep into the eyes. Time together brought us even closer than we had ever been before.

"See us then," I said, understanding that he would not need my assistance at the clinic but would not come home for the next few hours. Without time to wonder what might have happened, I turned back to Nicolas. We had been talking about making a new event for more people in the community. Since he was the organizer for this year, he was willing to make any necessary arrangements.

"What about booking that local here?" He showed me a villa that stood in the middle of the forest. It was never easy to find a place that was completely sealed off so that we did not have to look out of the window to see if people would come or see us. Furthermore, many of the visitors still studied and had limited economic opportunities. However, that meant that they would have a fast place in the past years, which they attended two times each. Unfortunately, the owner would die, and the new one was interested in everything but having us book a house on his grounds.

"It looks amazing, as long as there is no way through the forest right in front of it," I said while we opened a cart to check that out. Not that we would be doing anything illegal. It might just get too many curious gazes as somebody goes for a walk with his human pet. Pet-play is not very unusual, but one of my kinks was very sceptical of vanillas. Not as much as age-play, there was an adult who chose to be at a very young age while they made a session. Her or his dad or mommy would take care of her while that. Despite the fact that it's not always associated with penetrative sex and occurs between two responsible adults, it still faces significant criticism.

Lusie touched my behind, and I turned around at once. She smiled at me, eager to initiate conversation. I could see that. Fire bloomed in my eyes and chest. I excused myself and went to Andrea's cross with her. Since the clothing at such parties in general did involve much nudity, it did not take longer than a minute to make her stand fully undressed in front of me.

"Are you going to be a good girl?" My intense gaze made her smaller than she really was. Submitting me in every single way. "Of course, sir, I want to be your good girl." Her answer made me smile a little, while a mixture of feelings happened to surround me. Love, dominance, and desire

"Put your hands over your head," I commanded, and she immediately complied, backing away as I requested, while I moved closer to her until her beckon touched the cross. A short gasp left my tiny, sweet mouth, and it made my gut harden like stone. I had missed her. I had missed that. I would never let it go again.

While she stood there like that, I bent each of her arms to the sides of the cross. I had had a lot of training, and it wouldn't take me long at all to make a knot that she wouldn't be able to loosen by herself. Another gasp left her after she checked if she really was tied one hundred percent to it. Her eyes searched mine afterwards, finding me with lust that increased like a wildfire. Fast. Uncontrollable. Unstoppable.

In the room, there are about twenty people. In our case, it was just the two of us. Nobody else. With her, I could zoom out on everything. It was magical. It would never end while it was happening. Additionally, I could tell that it was the same for her, as her hungry eyes begged for more.

I handed myself a flogger. Even if I wasn't a sadist, I liked to use it to demonstrate that I was in charge. Others might want to see their submissive reaction; I only wanted their begging eyes, which longed for more. This connection was deeper than that of a typical relationship. The trust that lingered underneath increased with each session. It had been a long time since we had the last one. Exactly two years, I thought. That time with Nathaiel too. Intense. His commands were heartwarming and I eagerly followed them. I already felt that even my heart was not eager to stay in my body. People passed me like I was a train station. Even she wanted to move on to the two people she adored.

In the end, I loosened the rope and buried her back among the others. She would lean in closer and clench her fist as if she were in dire need of the physical contact. May she did; it had been such a long time for her that she did touch anybody. Even if we were in an open relationship, she had clearly stated that there had been no time or desire for anything on campus. Her sexual life would be limited to two meetings with us each year. Specifically, she would only engage in sexual activities with others during one of these meetings. She may not have told us what she did under her own duvet, at least not yet.

The evening was filled with laughter, warm conversations, and hot sessions in front of everybody. Lusie remained leaning towards me, watching some other people while talking to those who sat around us. I could tell that she not only wanted to have contact with me, but also that she had become a little tired. Of course she had. Her day started very early and was filled with many new events, which would surely leave her in need of time to think through everything.

It did, luckily, not take longer than half an hour before the first people started to leave. I brought her to bed, even though she wanted to help. However, she has a long day tomorrow. I would do the clean-up with some of those who remained to help. It was a relaxed mood. Even if almost all of them were tired, they would not stop wanting to have an amusing conversation while laughing and dancing while cleaning.

At half eight the next day, I woke up alone. Lusie and Nathaniel had disappeared again. Or did he ever get home yesterday? I decided not to wait for him since it was not sure that he would come at all, depending on what happened at the clinic.

"Good morning? Did you see Nathen today?" I asked Lusie, who was again deep into paperwork downstairs. Her face lit up as she saw me, but she would shake her head at my question. Who the hell was he? What could have been causing him to disappear for hours? "I will be eating some breakfast now, but I will drive to the clinic in around fifteen minutes. Do you want to join me?" I asked her, and perhaps she would have declined the food invitation if not for her stomach, which betrayed her. She had to eat. The last time she ate was at the clinic yesterday, and she wouldn't be in the mood for it either. Too much suspense and new events surrounded her, distracting her feelings.

At the clinic, nothing unusual had happened. Yes, Nathaniel had been here yesterday, but they said that it was only for an hour. I tried to call him. First time, no answer. The second time, nothing happened. I would call him later. Maybe he just needed some time off. Nathaniel never needed some time for himself. A voice inside me said something, but I had to ignore it. We have our usual morning meeting now. Today, with five newcomers, it was crucial for me to be available both mentally and physically. Just the usual routine. Just new people. Everything had to end well. It had to. Without him...

"Good morning, everybody. I am delighted to see our new joiners," I said enthusiastically while they sat down beside their guides for the week. Some had red eyes and were slightly sleepy, while others were restless and agitated. That would change. Soon. They just needed time. They are now here.
"If we start with what disappointments you had yesterday," I opened up for the conversation and, at once, three hands were up in the air, wanting to share it.

"I dreamt of my wife, and she was drunk in a bathtub filled with wine," one of the older patients said, but I remained calm. "Can you imagine why you dreamt about that?" I asked him, and he shrugged at first, not wanting to tell me anything. "Maybe because it always upset me that she would fill it too much and my own not understanding of that, she refused to drink herself. Even a tiny glass of wine, she would not share with me. Eventually, she left, and I consumed more than just that small glass of wine. Despite the provocation from both sides, his gaze remained fixed on mine, possibly searching for any hint of pettiness or harm in the story. They would not find what they wanted anyway; I had learned to remain professional. However, I refuse to allow their actions to significantly impact my personal life. In the end, they would go, and I would stay.

The next one was one of the youngsters, who surprised me by wanting to say anything at all. For me, at his age, it would have been rare to be at such a place. Indeed, I had experienced similar withdrawal symptoms before. However, despite the presence of approximately a hundred patients, I didn't even attempt to seek attention. Usually, I was blending in with the crowd, so why would I make an effort to stand out and gain acceptance?

"My girlfriend betrayed me as soon as I left yesterday," he said, evoking a mixed feeling inside me. I knew the feeling very well. However, I had come to understand that it held no significance because I had placed my trust in Lusie. I had even more sex than she had with other people. Still, it was not about the physical event; it was about the love that was between us. Nobody would ever reach that level with me. It would always just be who I adored now.

"What makes you feel that you have been betrayed? She still is a single individual, even if you chose to share some wonderful moments together." I opened up for a breath, thinking where her feelings were coming from. No answer. His fists flexed, and I knew that we would not get further if I did not turn the spell around.

"You know, I had felt exactly the same before many times," I explained, and Lusie looked at me in the moments I had judged her for her own sexuality. There was nothing she could change. For a considerable period, I remained oblivious to the element that enhanced her enjoyment of the moment. Until then, a lot of struggle with myself lingered inside me.

"She has been mine for three months. I cannot understand why she would do anything like that to me. Especially now that I had to leave, his gaze dropped to his hands, which no longer flexed. We would talk later. Just the two of us. Man to man. That might be the best. It was uncertain whether he would get the opportunity at home.

My phone started to vibrate in the middle of our morning routine. Normally, I would just hang up. However, as I saw the number, I had to excuse myself. That was important.

Chapter 7

"Okay, thank you. What about continuing with what you achieved yesterday?" I smiled, as I felt a little lost while I did not know eighty percent of the patients in the room. Whoever it was which had called Deen, it had to be important. Otherwise, his leaving was bothering me a little. However, I could do that. I had been preparing myself for these five years, and now I was more than capable of doing it in the best way possible.

"I sang on the stage yesterday, obviously. However, it had not been imaginable to see me on any stage again a month ago. I used to love it, but now the public wants a show, or at least good music. Imagine that it wouldn't be delightful if I was too drunk to even appear at my shows," he explained while smiling and nodding politely and understandingly. It delighted me a lot that there were not only the grownups who were used to that morning conversation, but also my department, which raised its hands to say anything.

"I slept," Ruth said shortly. Her hair was purple like a flower's, and with her green eyes and blue rings under her eyes, she was not anybody you would pass on the streets and forget at once. At least you would recognise her.

"Do you want to explain why that has been hard for you in the past?" I questioned her, uncertain if it was something she wanted to express in front of such a large crowd. Young people often turn to alcohol as a means of gaining attention and acceptance. A low self-worth, or just not considering how much it is going to damage you, did not just harm one teenager.

"I am just not used to that. I just…" She got uncomfortable, and it was right before I wanted to release her by saying anything to move attention away from her answer, before she let it out.

"At home, whether I sleep or dream, the acting in the room will be the same." Therefore, I cannot sleep." Tears swelled up in her eyes, and I told her that we would talk a little more about that after the morning session here. Together, more patients wanted to explain an achievement. It wasn't anything unnatural or understandable anymore. At the end of the meeting, Deen appeared again.

"I am sorry for my abstinence. However, we can move forward to free-time actions, and we are sure to split up the departments again." A hidden question lingered inside. Yes, I had a plan and didn't need his assistance. Therefore, I agreed with him at once and went upstairs with my youngsters.

"I heard you are going to make a tour throughout the building with Mrs. Johnson now. "In between, I am going to catch some of you for a short conversation so that I finally get the chance to know you better and not just listen to what your parents want me to know more about you," I explained, and they accepted it. Naturally, they are present, intelligent, and aware of the hidden meaning behind my gentle words. Still, they just nodded and left it like it was.

"How are you feeling today, Ruth?" As she followed me into my office, I asked her. It was a little exaggerated to call it that. Surely, I would not work there more often than in private conversations. Two cosy sofas facing each other and a larger table with six chairs adorned the space. Ruth looked somehow very relaxed, more than it was normal by just having stayed here for one day.

"I am very well; just the headache doesn't want to leave me," she smiled kindly at me, and I wondered if she meant by that her desire to come home as soon as possible and be "clean" or that she just enjoyed being here. She was difficult to read because she seemed to be using exactly the same strategy as me. Smiling. Always look happy and delighted so that nobody knows what you truly are feeling.

"That is good to hear, Ruth. It appears to me that you enjoy yourself here." I opened up for an open conversation, and she didn't hesitate to take the opportunity to start talking.

"Yes, they are all very adorable. This applies not only to your colleagues, but also to the children present. It feels lovely to be around here, and already now I am looking forward to the next Friday event," she explained, and I noted calling the others "kids," which was not normal while she was a teenager herself.

"You already have somebody to talk to, I saw," she said, not stopping to smile. I did not break the ice. I hated it. What would someone have to say to me so that I would start to trust them more? I pondered and eventually came up with a question known as an icebreaker. Soon, she would feel that I was not only interested in who she was now but also in how she got to be the person she is. "Tell me about your childhood; was it complicated like mine, or did you have a beautiful one?" I asked, at once assuring her that it was not anything unnormal for me to hear and know about a hard past. Her smile stopped. Her mouth popped open as her honest eyes met mine, but no words came out. The ice I was desperately trying to break worked. Finally, but hopefully not before, I could reach the safe land once more.

"I grew up with my dad and his new wife. She is the best stepmother you can imagine. She began, "The only thing that has always been rare was the fact that she is so young," to which I listened silently without passing judgment on anyone, as my knowledge of the subject was too limited.

"Dad would not be home often; therefore, we would make our evening beautiful without him. We really enjoyed ourselves," she said while nodding towards me with a smile. She assured me that her statements were accurate and reasonable.

"However, she started to be away one day for a reason I do not know." Her first seemingly happy gaze changed in a second to another, which was indescribable, lost, and sad. "While she was away, her dreams started. I could not control them." There was almost no difference between her beginning to cry and her current state. **Almost** nothing.

"I never remarked on it. Blood in my bed once, I thought, meant just that I had forgotten my bleeding. You know, things can vary greatly at the beginning. She looked into my eyes again for a short moment, but I did not nod. I did not let it go like a blind frog across the street. That would never end well; however, by remaining unsatisfied, I made her continue freely. We have now reached the most challenging part of the narrative.

"The funny part is that it was not me who slept there every night, since I had no allowance to be at any other place anyway. It was my best friend, whom he may have forgotten would sleep at our place." No more word was needed; already now her voice was shaky while her eyes were filled with tears. "Since then, I've known why I had those dreams." I cannot tell if everything was a dream at all. Every morning, my room appeared as if I had abandoned it before going to bed. I just... I just hated it." Her words said nothing in comparison to what she truly felt. That is what I knew.

For the rest of the day, I talked with every one of my patients. Those who underwent the withdrawal process would always remain employed. The others had every problem, from wanting to belong to a decent group to family struggles or childhood traumas. It was almost something I looked forward to, as I had had a conversation with everyone and would go on with the cancer patients. They, too, were the people I wanted to talk to. I primarily sought to understand the reasons behind the cancer's onset and to help them feel more at ease in this environment.

"Hi, how are you doing?" As I went into his room, I asked. He has been involved in sports since he was three years old, participating in activities ranging from running to ski jumping. Despite possessing multiple talents, he ceased his activities following the diagnosis two weeks ago.

"As fine as I get, I guess," he said while pushing himself to sit up. Still, one of his arms was broken, and he had been falling on a streetway while going out with his friends. It was maybe even luck for him, since they would diagnose him after that with bone cancer. Although rare, it remains a common conversation among teenagers about that illness.

"You look beautiful today." The sudden compliment hit me by surprise, but I just continued to smile while I thanked him shortly. It did not take me longer than a second to go on with the next question. As he reminded me of horny high schoolers, the most upsetting thing in my life, not only at the clubs Elisa desired to visit but also while I was simply riding the bus, I reasoned that he was possibly being a nice person.

"Your sports have to occupy your childhood, hasn't it?" I posed this question to him, but he simply shrugged, indicating he was not in the mood to discuss it. Immediately, I wanted to know more.

"I have to admit that I am not such a big sports fan nor enthusiast myself; however, I have worked with many who told me that it was taking them up badly every single day". "If it kind of is not your hobby," he cut me off, like he exactly felt what I meant, "then it will be an unbearable pressure to bear on your shoulders each day." I nodded and agreed with him. That was it. Again. No more words. I hated the silence after he started our conversation like that, but luckily it wasn't me who had to continue.

"I have loved sports since I was young. However, throughout the years I got also interested in other kinds of things." I did not want to know what that was, but could, depending on his external, imagine it already "My father also actively participated in sports. He never made it to become famous with it since he stopped at the age I am in now. Therefore, he kept telling me that it would go over soon, and I kept on training every day while having a competition one to two times a week," he explained, and I could tell what this was going to mean. He was torn between enjoying something and wanting to be a normal teenager with plenty of rest and leisure time. It was a hard decision, especially if you had already come that far with your carrier. He would already do it not only within the country, but also against others.

"What did you feel after getting the diagnosis?" I asked, and he shrugged again. It was a subtle provocation, but I interpreted it as the result of rarely engaging in conversation due to sports.

"I have never been afraid of death or injuries; otherwise, some of my sports would not be smart to do. However, as soon as I understood, my father assured me that it would only be a temporary halt, and I would recover within two months. I pondered whether I should take this as a challenge or a sign of respect from him.

We already had a plan for his treatment; in addition to the diet, he would get traditional Chinese medicine practiced with needles, called acupuncture. Be after the fathers wish, but also the best way of making his body even stronger. Engaging in regular physical activity within the limits of what is comfortable and safe can help improve mood, reduce fatigue, and maintain muscle strength and flexibility during treatment. Additionally, other supporting therapies such as massages, aromatherapy, and music therapy may provide comfort, relaxation, and relief from symptoms, at least for the time being. Nathaniel's task is to devise an operation plan, or whatever way we intend to remove it. He has more experiences, and even if I were to tell him my ideas, I trusted more in his knowledge than anybody else's, including myself.

"We will do our best to make you healthy again; however, what you want to make afterwards, we can support you with, but not make any final decisions for you," I explained to him while he tiredly nodded and seemed a little depressed. He had the right to exist. I didn't want to influence any of their decisions, even though I generally disliked making them. However, that was between having a professional career and wanting to be a normal kid, who would just enjoy and take life as it was.

"Lusie, would you come out for a second, please?" Deen appeared suddenly, almost surprising me that he would make his way to me, even if he had not been very supportive at the start of my career.

"What happened?" I asked, as once we were in a "safe" place, nobody else could hear us.

"It is about Nathaniel," he said, and my heart started to beat in the rhythm of a speeding train rushing down the tracks, racing ahead with a thunderous rhythm. What could happen to him? I did not want to lose him already. A thousand questions went through my mind before he got the chance to complete his sentence. What would happen with me and the clinic if he wasn't here anymore?

Chapter 8

It was nothing crucial, just a misunderstanding about some new treatment methods. Therefore, I was already on my way home, half an hour later. At least that had been my plan. She was not a person who was easy to forget, and maybe that was the only reason why I did recognise her once I left the building. Never had I thought that I would ever see her again, nor that this would be here in that case.

"Lena?" I looked a little sceptical at her, but her face lit up when she saw me.

"You" was the only thing she said, clearly not knowing my name, as I had gotten to know her during a period when it was off-limits. However, she had changed a lot, which I recognized. If she had been thin before, it seemed as though she had lost the last few kilograms since I met her. Her eyes were teary, with a prominent blue-green line underneath. She had not been sleeping or eating in weeks. It was painful for me to think about her.

"What happened? Why are you suddenly here?" I offered her my jacket, as her clothing was not suitable for the cool night. I insisted on her taking it after noticing her shackling and her body's discomfort.

"I...I... I don't know how to explain." Her voice was a mixture of stammering because of the freezing and not finding the right words. Surely, she had neither the energy nor the will left to allow her brain to function normally. "You are coming with me. Now. I am not going to leave you behind like that." I guided her to my car, and, to her luck, she did not try to turn around.

On the way, I got her a pizza, which she would have to eat if she wanted me to let her go anytime soon. Slowly and unsure, she obeyed. Still, I wondered what had happened to her and why she came to me instead of anybody else.

We came half an hour later to the garage. In the car, she had been fighting with herself not to fall asleep. As a result, I had not talked to her because I wanted to give her a little break.

I offered, "You can sleep and rest here that night, and tomorrow we can figure out anything," but she backed away, as if there might be something that could harm her. Therefore, I had to ask. Even if I liked to help people, putting myself at risk was not something I wanted.

"Are you running away from anything?" These were a few words that carried significant meaning in various directions. Still, she laughed out loud for a second while shackling her head.
"If so, I am the person who is running behind." I looked deep into her eyes as I tried to figure out what she meant. Who would she want to see again? Of all the people I had seen her chattering and laughing with, there was only one whom I had remarked as special for her. Jake.

"I haven't seen nor heard a word from him since I left. It was Lusie who stayed for two more weeks and would tell me that he said that it was the last time we saw him." I explained the information firmly, neutrally, and rationally. Her eyes widened for a second, as she may have been surprised that I figured everything out in the course of two seconds. I didn't get why people always thought that was such a special rarity. It says more about our society than about me. Observing simple facts and being good at connecting them was really no magical action.

"He wouldn't leave before he assured himself that really nothing was left of him," she explained, and I wondered why she would say so or if he would do anything like that. Never had I asked him about where he came from; always had I remarked that he did not want to pick up such themes. I don't ask anything without a purpose. He was my only friend from further away; why should I want to know anything that made me want to be in that kind of relationship? It was evident that he had not pursued his work and education in a conventional manner. I knew the high society well; nobody was his father to whom he legally, or better yet, officially, belonged. The next thought I had to skip was that it would say too much about vulnerable themes.

"Why do you want to find him if he's not looking for you?" I asked her, already imagining an answer or at least having an idea why that would be the way.

"I…it… I don't know. It is complicated," which was the easiest way of indirectly saying that they are in love, or at least she is with him, but that anything doesn't work like it should. The fact that he had a secret past convinced me, which I did not like. Not at all. I had two choices: help her with the negativity of getting to know more about who my former friend was. Alternatively, I could choose to allow her to stay while protecting myself by not offering any assistance.

"Who was Cecilia? They had never been in love." There I passed the last way out I had. Now, everything might ruin the appreciation I had for him. I liked the guy; he was so easy to talk about themes that others ran away once they heard a single word. On the other hand, exactly that quality might be the curse of what he had seen, heard, or even done much worse than that. We humans were born scared. With every single action we take or see being taken, we change. That can make us even more frightened, but if we are always in charge, it can also go the other way around. I was afraid that this might be the case for him.

"He never told me a lot," she started, and I began to count the details that supported the idea that he wanted to protect her and us while not explaining a lot about him. Despite our familiarity with him, we were unable to provide any additional information about Jake to our enemies.

"Is his name the real one?" I asked her, and her eyes widened, while my questions may have overwhelmed her a little. It was just what came through my mind; I couldn't do anything against that. If she wanted me to assist her, I had to gather information about what nobody expected. If he truly went undercover from now on, he would spend a long time searching for what he wanted others to consider first.

Her eyes showed me the pain she had been going through not only since his disappearance, but also long before, as they sat beside each other but were still miles apart. It made me wonder why he would let her come that close at all. Obviously, it might be hard for him to let her go. On the other hand, wasn't it even more difficult to have her by his side when he couldn't touch her or even speak to her like a regular person?

"I am sorry that I came here; I don't know what hit me. Somehow, I thought you knew more about it," she explained, almost on the way to leave. "Stay," my voice cut through the air, making her at least stand still. She would not go anywhere. There were three things she had to do now: eat, sleep, and search for Jake **with** me, so that I could possibly protect her on that journey. Why would I do that? That was easy. He was torturing himself while holding her at arm length, or now even further. Still, somehow, I was his friend. He had aided me on three occasions: once in the pharmaceutical industry, once during Deen's disappearance in Dubai, and perhaps most importantly, he was the driving force behind our current relationship. Not only had he been guiding Lusie through the first main steps she needed to know, but he also helped Deen accept his sexuality the way it was. It was just a simple, nice gesture to help him now, too.

The next time I looked at the watch, it was five a.m. She had been sleeping while I was desperately trying to learn more about the new case I started. Lusie's avoidance of social media calmed me, even though he had never used it before. Two different reasons may even contrast with each other. Being too poor to start with it and reject it later out of the reason to not want a life for the word but for yourself, against being wealthier and more powerful than the official richest man, but having to hide yourself for not being seen by your enemies. A shudder ran through my spine at the last thought. I think it was the first time that I dwelled on my former decisions.

"You are here," she said, waking up and explaining the obviousness of the rare fact that I did not leave. At least it did not sound like I would just "vanish" from a party for my job and end up with a woman in the garage. You could turn it around in every way you wanted; however, I had to contact someone who may already be missing me. Later. Not now. I was too focused on my search for Jake to hold other "normal" conversations about anything else. "Did you find anything?" she inquired as she carefully approached the computer, taking care not to make any mistakes.

"I know where we can possibly find more information. However, I am not good at cyber research, so I don't know how much." I couldn't end my sentence before she had her arms around me. It took me by surprise, but I let her, even if I was not a big supporter of such interactions.

"Thank you. You are really my hero." I tried to turn her enthusiasm down, but before I could say another word, she already ran out the door with my jacket. There was nothing important in it, and I may even have offered to give it to her since she didn't have anything herself, but it took me by surprise that she would just take it. She would disappear in the next moment.

I looked at the screen again. It was nothing special. At least for me. If she knew anything further, it might be a code too. There was just a simple sentence that was pointed out: "Nobody comes from nowhere." It was obvious on one side, but rare, as it doesn't say anything but that there is actually a place on this earth where his mother gave birth to him. Nothing else. We all know one thing: we will always be here, alive or dead. We will always leave something behind. It can be a huge business or a single footprint that never disappears. Ever.

"I am fine, Lusie. Calm down." Deen had been calling me multiple times, and I noticed that once I got back to the clinic, my phone lay still. As I left the house again, I had forgotten it. While I was at the garage with her, I would completely forget about it. Apart from the clinic's responsibilities, my sole motivation for returning was to bring the small items with me.

Still, it bothered me that I had not reached anything in the past few hours while she went away. No more details or coordinates would help someone like me understand the situation. I had too little knowledge to be able to solve the four-word code. She knew it immediately; I saw it in her eyes and in the way she reacted. However, she was the only person who would ever see him again from us.

Chapter 9

I did not comprehend the fact that she had been here. Lena. The girl, who bore a striking resemblance to me yet remained distinctly different, was certain that Jake harboured feelings for her, yet we never exchanged words. Why would you leave whoever you love most? Why would you hurt someone whom you adore? People are rare, and there are no excuses for that. Even though it might be difficult, there is always a way to find them. However, there is a way for people who love each other to work. Always. In conclusion, I may have read too many books by Austen during my alone time.

"Is there anything we could improve about feeling that we are not far away from each other?" I asked with all the innocence I felt at the time. Before Deen took the first step, Jake had already adopted a kinky lifestyle.

Nathaniel chuckled. I had not heard that often. "We will see; there are some hours left of the day before we can figure out anything." After he said it, the message was clear. Work. The only thing that didn't wait. Aside from death, of course.

Today, I would be more involved with cancer patients. My plan was to shift my primary focus each day. I planned to dedicate three days to withdrawal, three days to cancer, and the final day to office work. If you had started anything, that is how life would be. Of course, you could delegate some of your responsibilities to others, but that didn't guarantee that everything would proceed as I desired. I was not a control freak, however, and I still wanted to know that, especially at the start, everything went as I had planned for the past five years. That was important.

The day went faster than I had expected. The sportsman's father was in town, and now, after he had concluded his conversation with his son, I would confront him, accusing him of neglecting his training due to his cancer.

"Excuse me, would you have a minute?" We went into my office and sat on each side of the sofas so that we would be facing each other directly during this conversation.

"Is everything alright with the treatment?" he asked in shock. At once, we were sitting down. I looked him deeply in the eyes, trying to figure out if he was scared about his sports career or later life.

"Not completely. One factor increases a person's susceptibility to even the most basic illnesses. It also has a negative impact on cancer," I began, while his eyes remained focused intently. I wondered why he would push him into something if he himself knew exactly how hard it might be as a teenager. Yes, he would think about it differently now, but his son wouldn't.

"What do you mean?" He wasn't aggressive, but his fear made him lose a bit of control. I wouldn't do anything until he didn't put me in any kind of physical danger. It was neither unnatural nor voluntary for people to react in this way, placing themselves in an uncomfortable and shocking situation. Still, I didn't let his mood affect my desire to say what I wanted to him. Otherwise, it could or may even affect the treatment badly. That was nothing anybody wanted from us. Before that, we might have to ban him from going to his own son. People often underestimate the importance of the human body's response to stress. In certain cases, stress may even be the cause of illnesses like cancer. Naturally, I wouldn't mention it to him.

"You may have been at the point where the only thing you wanted was to be a normal teenager," I started, and he relaxed immediately while rolling his eyes like I had been fooling him already.

"That is just a period now. He enjoys sports and will be fine in a year, when he becomes a little more mature and understands the benefits he receives from them. Therefore, I felt compelled to clarify the situation for the benefit of my son.

"You might understand me wrong, but it is not the flu your son is here for. He had cancer. If we don't continue with our current treatment plan, there might not be an "in a year." The stress of getting as fast as possible healthy is not supportive at all," he looked at in shock at my harsh words. The truth was never easy, but it was the fastest and most understandable way to make him wake up from the dream he had about his son being a super athlete while he was on the verge of death.

"You are kidding now," he joked occasionally, while I remained professional and firm. No, I was not. Why should I? There was definitely a lot of other stuff to do, rather than "kidding" around with my patient's father.

Luckily, he understood that my remaining in the position meant that I did not mean it as a joke at all. He buried his head for a short moment in his hands before he was ready to confront me again. While he had been doing that, it was easy to see now that it was the crying, which almost started, that he had been trying to stop. Up until now, he had pushed away the thought of such an event for his brain's safety.

"What can I do? How can I help?" He asked me, and I started to smile politely, accepting his mood change more quickly than the reality of his son's sickness.

"Make him clear that it is his choice. Even if he decides to go ahead, he will have ample time to recuperate and contemplate, free from the burden of a task he's uncertain he can accomplish again. Now he nodded silently, while his eyes had turned red. The next thing he would do at home, I could tell, was to let everything out.

"I am sorry," he said in such a low voice that it was almost a whisper. I nodded and tried to comfort him with some assuring words, which meant as much that it would be fine as long as he relaxed here.

"What kind of father am I?" He was behaving strangely now, which made me fear that he had lost "himself" right in front of me. I could not tell if he would be ashamed of anything he might say or do now out of emotion. Therefore, I had to end this. If he needed help, I was not a psychologist. Yes, I had some words to share with him, which calmed him, but what such events could make is more anything, which possibly could curse psychological help over time. I was not educated for that. Neither had I the time here to share with him some more minutes of mine.

I stood up and told him that he would have to go now. Luckily, he understood it, and I immediately started to act. Slowly, but at least directly, he went out of the room while he tried to dry his tears quickly. Nobody would judge a father in such a situation. Still, I might give people a reason to feel pity for him, as he didn't seem like a man who enjoyed such situations.

"Thank you for the conversation. Would you believe that it is smarter to step into his room again now or tomorrow?" He asked, and I assured him that tomorrow was fine enough, depending on his primary position. Nobody needed him to cry in front of his son, while the child itself suffered from a sickness and needed no one else to see their worries beside him. He is not guilty of what they are experiencing. He couldn't do anything to change their feelings, nor could he do anything to cure them and become healthy again in a few months.

Before I continued my daily routine, I went into his room, where he lay there with his face tensed while I could imagine what he was thinking about. Tomorrow, I had the idea of bringing some of the other withdrawal patients in to see him. He said that he wanted to know how it was to be a teenager. Most of those who are here have at least been there before.

"I had a conversation with your father," I started, and his eyes widened in shock. Did I also see a little fear?

"Calm down; everything is fine. I told him to go home now, but he will be back again tomorrow to tell you the same as I am now, okay?" It was rare to see how he relaxed at once, as I said that his father was no longer here. Their relationship might be more complicated than I thought. However, as I sat there alone with him, he would be calmer than if he were here too. Is this a good or bad sign for me? It meant that my patient trusted me, and maybe even appreciated or liked me as a person. However, it was concerning that he harboured such negative feelings towards his own father. Nobody should feel this way about their parents.

"We both want to make it clear that it will be your choice what you are going to do after your stay here at the clinic. How long it will take is uncertain, but I want to assure you that it will be fine if you relax more. Say what you would like to do, and we will try to make it possible. I had an idea about bringing some of the teenagers here with me tomorrow so that you can actually hear what you have missed." I winked towards him, and he laughed with a kind smile.

"Thank you." His words hit my heart more than they should have. It was a positive effect, but if anything would happen to him during the operation, it still did not have to be a good thing to have a relationship with his patients. Yes, I trusted in Nathaniel's treatment methods, but still, he always kept saying that the possibility was there. Always.

Later that day, I found myself undressed in front of Nathaniel and Deen. The most positive aspect of this situation was that my thoughts were focused solely on the primary action. Rather than reiterating the day's events, I listen to what I want to accomplish and contemplate how I could improve. Most of the time, that was not helpful anyway. We tend to place excessive blame on ourselves for events that have passed and are beyond our control. In the end, we should always know why we made our decisions. They will usually always be the best, since we do have time to consider them with our entire knowledge and experiences in that second. Everything that comes later makes us more aware of what our decision affected, but it does not give us the chance to change it anyway. Everything you once said will be long gone and unchangeable once it leaves your mouth. As a result, I liked it here. It was not my words; it was just my actions. Even with these actions, they were simply what he wanted me to do; there was no need for me to consider or understand the deeper meaning behind his instructions. He provided simple facts and instructions for me to follow. Nothing more.

Chapter 10

Sweat covered our bodies as we all arrived at the literary conclusion. The energy level is flashing red, indicating zero. Still, we would take a shower together while nobody said a word. The moment captivated us—a rare occurrence indeed. Nothing could separate the three of us from each other. Aside from this one thing, which was sure to hit us all someday. Not now. We had too much to experience before that.

We slept in and woke up, arms in arms. It was just four a.m., but we were all there, ready to start our day. Imagine that even Deen was not in a bad mood as often as everyone else.

Together, we cooked breakfast and laughed over various jokes. It was as comfortable and relaxing as imaginable. Even if I already began thinking fifty times—just half of the brain was in primary action while the other one was at work—it was still good to know that I was with them for longer than just a few minutes. Even if we worked exactly in the same places, it would seldom happen that I saw them more than twice a day. Most often, it was just a smile or a nod while we headed to the next goal.

"What about making anything special this Friday too?" It was only Monday, but Deen was already obsessed with what to do at the end of the week again. I understood it, since it was one of the best moments at the clinic; new patients arrived, while some healed and could leave the clinic, hopefully forever. It was amusing to consider that nobody wanted to see each other again. We had gone through a difficult period together, but that was the end of it. Following that, it was important to continue with your normal life; expect us, of course.

"It is not even five yet; who would join me for a walk throughout the park?" he asked, since we normally would not have the time after work anyway. We all joined in, but first we needed to get dressed better. Not much, but a little snow had been falling all night. I liked the winter; outside, it would always be quiet and calming, while sitting inside in front of the fireplace was wonderful too. It was delightful to hold a warm cup of tea in your hands as you gazed at the icy snow falling outside.

"What did you use to do as a child in the winter—a snowball fight or sledding?" As we went side by side, with me in the middle, I asked and threw the new snow that covered the ground. There were no cars driving past here. Only the footprints of the animals residing here were visible; we might have glimpsed a portion of them during our passage, yet the rest remained concealed and unidentified, despite being our nearest neighbours.

They said "both" and "nothing" in the same second, and you may be able to imagine which one of them said which.

"At school, we often had snowball fights, even as teenagers and sometimes at the college," Deen explained, while Natheniel shocked his head sceptically.

"I do remember the time it was ice inside, and you came home with a laceration too," they said, initiating a discussion about whether it was wise to have fun and take a risk or to choose something else. Nobody wan. In the end, reading or researching something inside was an option, but it was not convenient to have fun with the actual season. In the end, you could always do other things. I liked both ideas anyway.

"We go this way." Nathaniel turned towards the small gap, which was slightly longer but particularly wonderful.
In spring, the flowers bloom and birds sing as nature wakes from its slumbering. Summer brings warmth, blue skies, long days of sunshine, and new dreams. Then autumn comes with gold leaves, crisp air, and stories yet to be told. Each season dances in its own way on a colourful journey, day by day. We had not seen winter yet, but already, as I saw the snowflakes gently descend, blanketing earth in a shimmering blend, I could tell that it would be a huge concurrence.

Slowly, we went hand in hand with the wonderful winter. That was worth the earth. Nothing could compare to making it instead of As Nathaniel and Deen led me down the snowy path, their hands intertwined with mine, I couldn't help but feel a sense of warmth despite the winter chill. A blanket of white adorned the forest around us, the trees standing tall like silent sentinels guarding our journey. It was a picture-perfect scene straight out of a winter fairytale.

As we walked, our breaths formed clouds in the frigid air, mingling and dissipating into the ether. Deen's laughter echoed through the woods, infectious and full of life, while Nathaniel's calm presence grounded me like an anchor in the swirling storm of my thoughts.

Nestled among the trees, we discovered a small, quaint house, its smokestack releasing lazy tendrils of smoke into the sky. It seemed almost magical, as if plucked from the pages of a storybook. Nathaniel and Deen exchanged a knowing glance before guiding me towards it; their excitement was palpable.

Snowflakes covered the windows around us as we entered the cosy abode. The interior was simple yet inviting, with plush cushions scattered around and soft blankets draped over worn furniture.

Nathaniel and Deen turned to me as I sat by the small bank, their expressions filled with a mixture of nervousness and anticipation. My heart fluttered in my chest as I met their gaze, unsure of what was to come but trusting in the connection we shared.

"Lusie," Nathaniel began, his voice soft but determined, "we've been wanting to talk to you about something important."

I nodded, feeling a knot form in my stomach. Whatever it was, I knew it would change everything between us.

"We've been thinking a lot about our relationship," Deen added, his hand reaching out to grasp mine, "and we've come to realise that what we have is special. We love you, Lusie, more than words can express."

Tears welled up in my eyes at their heartfelt words, and the warmth of their love enveloped me like a cocoon. I had never felt as cherished and seen as I did in that moment.

"And we want to take our relationship to the next level," Nathaniel continued, his voice steady but filled with emotion. My entire body was shackled. What would they do, or did they really plan to start with what I had in mind?

I stood up, partially in shock at their words, but also to maintain a close proximity as they stood in front of me, and I sat on the small bank. However, once I had been standing, they would kneel down.

They said my name in the same second, "Lusie." My eyes filled with tears, wondering if that was reality or a dream again. It wouldn't have been the first proposal, but it was the first that included both of them. Was that even legal? While both of their eyes shone sincerely towards me, I wondered. My heart beats faster than a wild stallion racing across the open plains, fuelled by the fire of our love's unbridled passion.

"Would you want to marry us?" The words made a shiver run through me. Marriage. I'd never had the time to truly consider that. It was quite overwhelming, but at the same time, I didn't want to leave. How would the weeds even look alike? I had seen plenty with a couple, but never a trio. Would we even have a chance to do it here?

While a thousand thoughts ran through my mind, Nathaniel waited. Deen not. His voice was shackling; too much adrenaline was running through him.

"We understand if it's too much, Lusie," Deen said gently, his eyes full of understanding. "We just wanted to be honest with you about our feelings, and we respect whatever decision you make." Before he could continue, the word left my mouth, and the first tear of pleasure escaped from my eyes. I could never have anticipated such an experience during a morning stroll, or at any other moment.

"Yes," it was a whisper, while a smile started to spread on my lips. "Yes, of course, a thousand times yes," I said while Deen stood up and kissed me eagerly. I loved that action as much as my thoughts with Nathaniel—I would marry him too, yet he just would have to watch us now, or...

I felt his warm hand on my back while his head rested on the top of our heads. An honest hug while we both kissed. It was more promising than anything I could have imagined.

In that moment, it was not about us being a trio. No. It was a promise of being alike forever. Our love is bigger than anything else that could ever destroy that moment. Being one in every single passing second of our lives was a thought that warmed my heart, while the cold winter air got warmer, and summer surrounded us.

Like that, it happened on a cool winter morning on Monday. Before the rest of the world would wake up, we would already be thousands of steps away. Nobody could stop us. They could try; on the other side, they would surely recognise soon enough how little it made up. Nothing.

Breathless, our foreheads rested for a moment on each other while we both smiled. Could my life ever remain that fantastical? I think I have come to the best moment. Ever. Nothing could tear us apart; aside from that, don't ruin that now, mind.

"When will it happen?" I asked, and they both laughed at my eagerness. Of course, I was now eager; what did they expect? A proposal, and then continuing everything as it always had been. No. I wanted to hear the continuation.

"We will fly to China in three months. You can directly inquire about it on March 12th. The wedding is scheduled for the fourteenth, but we won't be returning before the twenty-fifth, he explained with his usual calmness and directness.

I started to laugh. "What would you have done if I said no?" I asked, and he shrugged while also showing a sexy smile on his lips.

"I knew you would say yes, but if you hadn't done that, I would have cancelled the wedding, but I still travelled with the two of you to China." Of course, he knew me well enough to understand my decision. It was perhaps one of the easiest I had ever taken.

Chapter 11

We were about to board the flight to China, and while I was looking forward to it, I couldn't help but feel irritated by everything going on at the clinic right now. To clarify, it is in my department. It's not that I didn't receive a sufficient number of requests; in fact, I received almost too many. I had to decline some of them because the capacity wouldn't be enough. Right now, the number of addicts is increasing, not decreasing, as I had hoped. There were so many addicted people. Didn't I have to cure everyone at once?

The worst part was that right now I had received a request from someone who had been here before. My treatment for two people had lasted between one and two months in total. Still, both of them couldn't bear it. However, my treatment was insufficient to help them overcome the trauma that had previously destroyed their lives. Still, I had to see them again, even if that was something I did not wish for at all.

It was such a demotivation that the first thing I did, as I was the familiar face, was to decline the invitation to come back again. I stopped myself at the overcrowded since I had at least checked out that I had enough places filled to give me the luxury of choosing between patients.

"It looks like someone wrestled with a mud monster and lost!"

Lusie suddenly walked into my office. I had been almost hiding in it for the majority of the day. Still, what I wanted to do wasn't fully finished. Too much time had gone by to think about what I had been doing wrong here.

"Very amusing." I didn't even look up at her as she entered the room with a smile and stepped behind me to look at the computer screen.

"You have more requests than I do," she remarked, and I was just on the verge of responding, fortunately. Children shouldn't be here. They shouldn't experience cancer or drug addiction at such a young age. It had nothing to do with Lusie or her idea, but it was heartbreaking for me to imagine that they too cast away such an important part of their lives while they thought of being undamageable, just because it didn't hurt the next day. What would the next day's pain be like? Nothing compares to how much you harmed your body over time. It felt much better to be sober.

"Mhh" was all I could say in response to her embrace, as she hugged me tightly. Her warmth made my mood unfreeze a little. Still, the inner feeling of not having done enough, not being enough, and making any mistakes that would come together increased. I was just a breath away from declining the other patients, who had been here before, too. However, Lusie started to go a step further, distracting me from the work I had to do before our journey.

"Tell me what it is that bothers you that much." She inquired, and I felt my face relax as I realized the depth of her concern for me. She was reminding me again how much I loved her and why I did it. A beautiful soul beneath a gorgeous body—what would be better? "They have been here before," I pointed out to the two people; I had already declined one of them. She frowned at it, taking a step away from me.

"Why did you decline him?" She asked, not really in wonder, but almost like she was blaming me for it. I started at once to come into a defensive position. I knew my action hadn't been right, but if I didn't help him the first time he was here, why would I do it the second?

"They have been here before and received the same treatment, which they would also receive a second time. It apparently did not help. They did take their drug again and want to come back to do the same thing over and over again. I don't appreciate it," I explained, my tone demanding yet slightly shaky. She leaned against the wall behind me, never missing our eye contact, desperately trying to understand my thoughts.

"How many times did it take for you until you started to understand and accept that alcohol wasn't good for you at all?" She questioned me abruptly, instilling a sense of confidence in me. Therefore, it would take me two seconds to get any kind of smart answer together.

"Too many," I began, but she cut me off. "How many?" she asked, and I started to count. The first time I counted was fifteen, followed by a second count a year later, and then another...

She kept looking at me while I was silent, trying to figure out the number. It was a long time ago. Initially, I would order them from my parents, then from Nathaniel, and ultimately, I would settle for the one I believed would be most suitable. The question was whether the others had been a waste of time, or if that final remark would never have come if they hadn't existed.

"See, I am not interested in the number, just the fact that you didn't do it the first time either." She came closer again to me while she looked deep into my soul. "Why would they be any better than you there? Think of it as a compliment: they liked your treatment so much that they would choose us again. To decline their try for a second chance is not only foolish but also a mistake," she explained before she turned around and left me again alone.

I sat there. A mistake. Yes, she was partly right, but on the other side, there are other people outside who wouldn't make such a *mistake*. Why I had been doing that was affected by many reasons. At first, I didn't find a sense of belonging or solace in the thought of not being as good as Nathaniel; later, I experienced the deaths of my parents; and finally, I struggled to accept my own sexuality, a process that took several more months.

On the other side, who was I to decide if they didn't have a reason that was "good enough" for making them back up again? If I did it, they could too. If I had a reason, whatever theirs was, it was also for them to start again with something they knew damaged them. If I needed further chances, why did I curse them for doing that too? For the rest of the patients, I pressed the accept button.

The next morning, we would all wake up at five a.m. again. In the past few days, we have started to make a routine out of it. We wouldn't necessarily pass the same way that we did three months ago at the proposal, but we would almost vary it daily, as much as was possible. Maybe I was getting old, but I enjoyed standing up earlier and making anything out of the day before starting work later.

"When are you going to pack?" Nathaniel asked the two of us as we went through the forest, which made it even darker than it truly was in March.

"We are heading away in two days, so maybe in two days, I guess," I said, eliciting a chuckle from Lusie. Nathaniel rolled his eyes, shackling his head in disbelief that I would push it as far away as possible.

"I already have laid some clothes to the side, which I think will suit well. However, what about the feast clothing?" Lusie gazed at him in astonishment, while I relished the opportunity to be a man, even if it meant wearing a suit and tie.

"I have already ordered yours and Deen's dress; it will be at our place before we check in." My eyes widened before I understood that he was kidding. Not even showing a hint of amusement, just stating it as a dry fact... I alternated between hating and loving it at different moments. Right now, it was almost amusing that I had believed that he would order me into a dress on the wedding day.

"I wonder if anything is going to change for us after that." Lusie's thoughts quickly shifted to a theme that I had been wondering about too. We were all consented-upon adults, yet it was not normal in the monogamous society we lived in. Yes, we had each other and the scene to share, but what if it would damage the clinic? There was no guarantee that there were some foolish people out there who did not understand that you do not have to love just one person at a time. Some might even blame you if you don't fit into their worldview.

"We will be fine," Natheniel said shortly, but behind the stable frame, I could hear a little uncertainty too. It was surely also something that he had been considering. Of course he was; he did think about everything at least a hundred times, and it appeared at least sometimes like that. It may still be the best thing to keep in mind. Everything would be fine. As long as we lived as a trio, everything had to be fine. There was nobody who should have hurt us for that. We wouldn't do that to them, either.

Chapter 12

With pity and a happy eye, I went towards the last Friday arrangement. I might have at least missed that. Fortunately, we had scheduled our flight back to ensure we could return on Friday, two weeks later. Today, my first cancer patient will get another. Our department had already completed the count of patients. Each week, we would get at least a new one for the withdrawals, which until now had been going completely fine. Yes, people needed a different count of time, but until now, there was always at least one who was more than cured, eager to finally get home again. There may not be an exact time value for the withdrawal itself, but it was easy to hear and see that people wanted to move on again with their lives, especially teenagers, who desperately tried to hide such wishes.

"Mrs. Amans, wait for me; I am not that fast already." I recognised the voice behind me and started to smile as I turned around.

"Hi, how are you?" I greeted the athlete, who would eventually find his way out of the clinic. During his stay here, I learned so much about the boy that I began to like his character very much. Perhaps this was due to my initial assumption that his thoughts were solely focused on sports, but it turned out that he had a diverse range of interests. I had maybe never heard of a young person who had that many interests, ideas, and dreams for the future. I found it fascinating to observe his transformation from a child to a man. The diagnosis and progressing of his mind that these could have been his last year, or even just months, made a lot of sense. You started to come into a situation that was in contrast to the normal "you just live once, live that one time" type of thing.

"I am alright, but I don't want to run at once. I still have some time left until I am standing on the sports field again, haven't I?" I smiled, delighted that he had found what he wanted to do for the rest of his life, or at least for these years, he was fit enough for it.

"You are saying that the normal teenage life is not for you?" I challenged him with a raised eyebrow. Throughout his stay, I had given him the opportunity to get a hint of how normal kids would live. He returned home from school without attending any kind of event or training.

"Well, it has the positive effect of giving you more time to educate yourself in other directions than just at school. Conversely, after a week of inactivity, I began to feel a strong desire to take action. I am just a person who needs to train a lot and am not able to live the lazy kind of teenager life," I laughed out as he judged those of the same age for not making much out of their lives. Whoever I had here would get the chance to go to several courses and meetings with the different types of people who might already have achieved anything or had, in general, an important story to tell them. That didn't have to be anyone from nowhere; there might also be some grown-ups from other departments who are in a physical state and want to share their knowledge.

"I will miss you, that I can say. However, that doesn't mean that I want to see you back here, alright?" He laughed and nodded at first, but then he took up his hand, pointing it towards me as if he had gotten an idea he wanted to share.

"Are you really sure about that? What if I become a professional athlete? Wouldn't it be exciting to visit your clinic once a year? He offered, and I smiled warmly. How could such a great idea come from such a young person? I didn't wonder if he meant it or not; throughout his stay, I had gotten to know him very well, and he never mentioned anything that he did not mean in the exact way he said it.

"I would be looking forward to seeing you again in that kind of position." We went towards one another and gave each other a hug. At his young age, the sport he had been doing shaped him at least as much as the size he already had. It was comparable to Nathaniel's, maybe even Taler's.

He laughed as he released me from his arms and said, "Don't make me cry now; we will see each other through the evening, and perhaps the next time I am here as a professional, all right?" In his eyes, I found a tear. He too had many feelings about that: being glad to become a healthy human again, but also saying goodbye to the time and conversations we had here. I have to admit that he had gotten some more minutes than others, while I just worked a little longer so that everybody would almost get the same time as me.

As the event began, we started with the clinic song. Deen had to hold his speech, and then everybody could stand up and start with the first lines, while each department would continue with their verses. We, too, had gotten to write the last one.

"The weather is not forever,

Whatever pressure, terror us brought.

Members of an adventure we are now.

Whenever, wherever, whoever

In our centre is pleasure now

We don't have to be a model,

Just come away from the bottle.

Will pass what once was normal,

Come away from the daily quarrel.

Press the throttle now with us.

The weather is not forever,

Whatever pressure, terror us brought.

Members of an adventure we are now.

Whenever, wherever, whoever

In our centre is pleasure now

Whatever mattered once, like a hammer it comes.

An answer of life's disasters, a new chapter had to start.

Like a sneaking panther, mastering it all.

Gather for an answer, what matters is to come away from it all.

No disaster the cancer was, we mastered it we all.

    The weather is not forever,

    Whatever pressure, terror us brought.

    Members of an adventure we are now.

    Whenever, wherever, whoever

    In our centre is pleasure now

In the youth department, we find our truth,

where courage and resilience are our youth.

With each step forward, we embrace our growth.

In this haven of hope, we find our worth.

Together, we rise, champions of our youth.

    The weather is not forever,

    Whatever pressure, terror us brought.

    Members of an adventure we are now.

    Whenever, wherever, whoever

In our centre is pleasure now

Through sleepless nights we all survive

May took us by surprise, there where no goodbyes.

Paradise gave us other highs, alive.

Survived the deeps there the knife once strife's.

Apologize, it is to nice to be alive for us"

For a while, the hall echoed the last word of the song. It was a true endorphin kick to hear everyone become a part of something so big. It had gotten that way. Something huge. It was one of the biggest things that captivated me, at least in my heart. This was true not just for me, but for each and every one of my future husbands.

Many people sang today. Two of them are from my department, but all together there are seven. Leaning back and listening to their words was a delightful experience, as the sweetest melodies often conceal the most bitter lyrics. It was illuminating how many talented people there were on this planet, but only a few of them would become known. Furthermore, those who lacked talent were not necessarily better than those who simply sang in their spare time. Finding a place in the public's eye was largely dependent on luck. The music itself could reflect the mood of the moment rather than the actual quality of the artists or their songs. However, if we started a talent show here, I was sure that we would give at least one patient a new kind of start after their stay here. They had been singing in the kitchen one day, and it was almost too sad to let anyone else hear.

"Let us move on to find partnerships for the next week." It was obviously that Deen loved to stand on the stage. With an honest smile, he skilfully chose his words, interspersing them with easy jokes and brief digressions. In the end, he was good enough to make everybody listen and feel like they were part of it, even if they did not necessarily have to go on the stage themselves.

"Altogether, five wonderful people, including the first departure of our new department's cancer patients," he explained to everyone, and cheering and clapping began. It was not only an important journey for me, but also because most of the patients spent a lot of time with us, desperately trying to give the youth a better start after their stay here.

The athlete stepped onto the stage with ease and successfully treated his patient for the past week. A girl his age was also suffering from cancer. However, she was more than just beautiful; she was also a well-known author. She had missed many classes and had already completed her education at a reputable college. Like him, she is also a real multi-talent. That was no coincidence. Once I read about her, I knew with whom I wanted to see her. They fit better together than music and dance. His charm and persona may captivate her heart, or they may at least stay friends. I was certain about that. He acknowledged me with a half-smile as he stood on the stage. I reciprocated the wink, causing him to smirk with a brief shake of his head. That would have been fun last week for my former favourite patient.

Chapter 13

There was more than just Friday's event, which was special today. At once, we headed home, and our clothing was out in less than a minute. We were soon to be married; even if that and our honeymoon would flood together, it was already something we all looked forward to. Lusie talked or asked about that at least twice a day, while Deen's eyes would always widen eagerly as she did that. Our morning routine has now suited us well. It felt like we were getting more time together than that, even if we just deposed it from evening to morning. Yet, we still use the entire capacity of our energy. It was noticeable how much that changed each of us after work.

Today was our last day at the clinic. I hoped that everything would be fine, since I had in mind what happened with my former clinic when I left it the last time. However, I had made sure about increasing the security while we were away. Additionally, we prohibited any new individuals from entering the area during our absence. As a result, all of the new patients' parents, friends, and other close relatives had to come today at the arrangement; otherwise, they wouldn't get the chance to see their loved ones for the next two weeks.

Lusie's lips touched his, while something inside me moved itself. I had almost forgotten that part, since it never showed any importance to me anymore, aside from the few times a day on the toilet. The event that happened now made me shiver in wonder. However, as surprising as it had been, it would happen again. It left me with twisted thoughts about what it would ultimately mean for me.

While they were continuing, I changed into a different outfit, ensuring that my working clothes did not interfere with my privacy. Even though I refrained from wearing the doctor's coat, I sensed a sudden shift in my mindset when I wore a black leather jacket and jeans. It was a fetish or any other routine that brought my head into the focus I needed for each single event.

I bound them together so nobody would have a chance to run away, even though their bodies were not an inch apart. The only thing they could do was stay the way I wanted. I bound their eyes with more material than usual. They become even more helpless. They now belong to me in every possible way.

With Lusie, I could feel some pain, while Deen didn't tolerate anything at all. Therefore, I had most often chosen to make a kind of brainfuck while they didn't know what touched them. Today, my plan was a little different. Deen may not have wanted to experience the pain himself, but he didn't find it alarming to consider the possibility that it could strike him, or even Lusie, when it hit the ground.

At first, their breathing increased, but after the first hit, it stopped, trying to figure out what or who would be next. I liked to be in charge. Even if I trusted both of them, it would have been torture, if not sexual, for me to sit in front of anybody without being able to move, see, or smell what might come. In some ways, the contact with each other made one side of them safe, but the other one was even more vulnerable and present for me. Before each session, I usually planned out what I would do as a dominant. Even if it was possible to make anything spontaneous, we did have limited time most often, and I wanted to get as much as possible out of it.

"Your flesh could be opened by the next hit. Who will be hitting next, you Lusie or Deen, and where will it be?" I made their minds go in as many directions as possible. BDSM is primarily focused on the mindset of the individual. It wasn't just about deciding on a position but also about navigating within it. Each of the parts got into another space, which included not only the dominants or submissives but also every pet or age player, cuckolder, rope bunnies, sadists, masochists, and every other niche.

Ultimately, I allowed Deen to use it for its intended purpose. I let him choose where he'd like to use it. Watching them go through the process felt like therapy for me. While they were doing it, the memories of my childhood finally faded. My mind had recognised that just being here was no danger for me. I wondered if it would be ready for the next step, too. However, until now, it was enough to see how Deen chose to fill every hole in her.

The following morning, we started our walk again. It was the first day that we would repeat our paths completely alike. Additionally, we went into the abode, which Deen and I had proposed to her. It was relaxing to be back, while images of her heartwarming smile and tears of pleasure in her eyes came back to mind. It was maybe the most beautiful thing I had ever seen.

When we were there again, I opened up the papers on my phone. Usually nothing special; unfortunately, wars that had started, paused, or ended, politicians that had given some kind of critical statement, new businesses that had started and showed themselves as successful, or just the sports of curse.

Today was not like that. My eyes widened at the first headline I read: "Is the new natural healing clinic more efficient than our familiar pharmaceutical industries?" At once, I jumped up and went to Deen and Lusie, who were eating breakfast together and chattering about anything in the clinic. It didn't matter right now. This is good news. Despite the potential harm from our biggest concern, the initial words sounded promising.

"Look at this," I said to them, and they were both surprised at the new article. On one side, it was obvious why, but on the other, it was a little sad that they didn't write who the narrower was; aside from that, we knew the papers. I wondered if I knew the person, or if it had been here in the clinic or at the case last year. I couldn't believe that someone would take such a risk without any prior knowledge or interest.

"Did you know of any journalists or other patients who might have been interested in giving us such support?" When I asked Deen, he eagerly smiled, acknowledging that someone had shared this, while he struggled to identify the source.

"Of course I did, but we might as well read what's standing there before praising it." He remained more rational than I was, as the moment of enthusiasm caught me. That was what I always wanted: getting people to think about and choose wisely.

Is the new natural healing clinic as efficient as our familiar pharmaceutical industries?

In recent years, there has been a noticeable shift in healthcare towards embracing natural healing methods as a viable alternative to conventional pharmaceutical interventions. This shift is not merely a trend but a reflection of growing evidence supporting the efficacy and safety of natural healing practices compared to traditional pharmaceutical approaches. As the shortcomings and side effects of pharmaceutical medications come to light, more people are turning to natural healing clinics for solutions that prioritise holistic well-being over symptomatic relief.

Statistics reveal a concerning truth about the pharmaceutical industry: over the past decades, there has been a steady rise in the prevalence of adverse drug reactions and medication-related complications. According to a report by the American Medical Association, adverse drug reactions are estimated to be the fourth leading cause of death in the United States alone, resulting in thousands of fatalities annually. Furthermore, the over-prescription of antibiotics has led to the emergence of drug-resistant bacteria, posing a significant threat to public health worldwide.

In contrast, natural healing clinics offer a refreshing approach that focuses on harnessing the body's innate ability to heal itself through non-invasive and gentle interventions. Treatments such as herbal medicine, acupuncture, chiropractic care, and nutritional therapy are tailored to address the root cause of health issues rather than merely masking symptoms. Furthermore, studies have shown that natural remedies often have fewer side effects and are better tolerated by patients, resulting in improved treatment outcomes and patient satisfaction.

One notable advantage of natural healing clinics is their emphasis on prevention rather than reactive treatment. By promoting lifestyle modifications, dietary changes, and stress management techniques, these clinics empower individuals to take control of their health and reduce their reliance on pharmaceutical medications. This proactive approach not only fosters long-term health but also alleviates the burden on healthcare systems by reducing the incidence of chronic diseases and hospitalisations.

Furthermore, the rising cost of prescription medications has become a significant barrier to healthcare access for many individuals. Natural healing clinics provide a cost-effective alternative by offering affordable treatments and personalized care plans that prioritize patient well-being over profit margins. In a world where healthcare affordability is a pressing concern, this shift towards natural healing represents a beacon of hope for those seeking accessible and sustainable healthcare solutions.

The newest natural clinic's statistics impress us as being much better than the former opponent in court, Fav. Pharmaceutics. Since they are only specified in cancer and withdrawal treatment, these have shown up in an astonishing number of 96% of healthy patients after their treatment. This figure deviates from the industry's 43% cure efficiency in the previous year, indicating that only half of the new entrants achieve this.

In conclusion, the emergence of natural healing clinics marks a paradigm shift in healthcare towards a more efficient, safe, and patient-centred approach. By addressing the limitations and side effects of traditional pharmaceutical interventions, these clinics offer a holistic alternative that promotes well-being at both the individual and community levels. As more people recognise the benefits of natural healing, we can expect to see continued growth and innovation in this field, ultimately leading to a healthier and happier society.

"That was really good." Once I finished reading, Deen praised it. My heart beats like a triumphant elephant, and too many endorphins run through my spine. It was a long time ago that I felt such happiness after a success. That was definitely one.

To hear that we would take the flight later today was both a wonderful goodbye gift, but it also made me shiver at the thought that we were standing on the most harmful side of them, and with that, we were what they wanted to destroy. On the other hand, I hoped they were not stupid enough to make it twice. The article's release coincided with the conclusion of the case less than a year ago. This time, there wouldn't be any doubt about who would have done that. Additionally, just the attempt would be seen long before it happened. I had learned from my mistake. It had been the last one.

Chapter 14

We laughed and cheered, while the article's release surprised me in a positive way. Day one of our journey started almost as a wedding gift, and I wonder how it would continue.

Right now, we are stepping into the car on the way to the airport. The mood was even better than it had been on our walk earlier this morning. Nathaniel, too, was so easy going and relaxed after reading the news that it was evident he too loved the event. Of course he did; in the end, the entire clinic thing was his idea, while the size of how it was now was Deen's. It happened unimaginably fast, even if it took a few years. The process seemed to move much more quickly than expected. The only thing that had slowed down our progress was my studies, but we would catch up in the years we had left.

"That's the wrong way," I said at once. Nathaniel drove out an exit too early. He didn't even react; therefore, I looked upon him in wonder while I raised an eyebrow, waiting for an explanation or an answer.

"It is not," he said simply, and I leaned back while trying to figure out where he wanted to drive us too. In the mirror, I could see Deen, who sat behind us in the middle, desperately trying not to start laughing.

"What is so amusing?" I asked, frowning, and looking more desperate around me, before I realized what he was laughing about, and why this wasn't the wrong exit,

We managed to feed our family for nearly a year, all the while keeping up with our apartment's rent. Maybe little James even could have gotten the tiny car he always wanted to play with, but we never had enough money to pay for it. Around ten private jets stood there, waiting for anybody to be used to them. I folded my arms in front of me, continuing to wonder if that was a positive thing or not. The last time I insisted on taking the public aeroplane was years ago. In some ways, I had gotten used to allowing myself some more benefits while still not having to work as hard as I had done while living with Elisa. It was simply a new chapter in my life. I pursued five years of further education at the world's top medical university. Now, we are steering our own department at our clinic and not "just" cleaning it. Indeed, I was no longer working as frequently. Yet, my mind was at that place more often than it had been before. My spare time was captivated by thoughts of what I could do better to increase status and productivity, while also considering the long time the patients needed to cure.

"Are you going to fly with us, or do I have to bring you to the public aeroplanes since it is such a crime?" Nathaniel asked calmly, noticing that I knew exactly where we were going.

"I don't know yet," I explained, and he laughed for less than a second. I wondered if he was laughing about me or the fact that this was such a complex choice to make. It was not what he wanted. No decision was complicated for him.

"You will have to consider that quicker; we are driving in there and starting at once after that. No hours of waiting or a thousand check-ins to go through before we take off," he explained, and I recognised the benefits he had been missing while obeying my wish to not take such an expensive private thing earlier. He had been doing it just for me since Deen was more than open to the idea of having some luxury.

"Since you are taking it anyway, I think it would be stupid to reserve another seat on another airplane. I may join in," I accepted, and his smile increased. While he said "good girl," he let me feel like this was a test or a part of a session.

"Additionally, we are skipping flight time too, so we aren't going to get through the game of life this time," Nathaniel explained calmly, while Deen's eyes widened in anticipation of getting another chance to play this game, which we had been doing on the last flight to China.

The plane itself was not filled with any unnecessary details. It's almost simple, with luxury seats and different rooms to choose from. Our crew consisted of three men and a woman. The pilots there, both male, greeted us as we stepped in, but we wouldn't see them for the rest of the journey. The stewardesses there, from each gender, were very polite, and already, as we stepped in, they were confronting us about whether we wanted anything before the take-off. We sat at a table where we could face each other and have a table in between us. Of course, just to earn some distance... No, we would make Deen's dream of giving him a second chance at that game come true. However, we didn't start before the plane was in the air. Until that moment, I was leaning against the window, looking out at our small earth while we were thousands of hundreds of kilometres over it. I would have waved goodbye if I hadn't known that we would see it the entire time and in some hours be just on another place, but on the same earth again.

"I am going to be a musical artist," Deen chose as the first choice, not wanting to educate himself any further at the start of the game.

"I take the longer way," Nathaniel said, wanting to educate himself more again. Now it was my turn. What would I do? I liked my current job a lot, but last time I remembered Nathaniel avoiding it because it would have been the pharmaceutical influence in the game. Even the simplest choices showed our mindset very well. As I didn't like decisions in general, this was not what I adored most.

"I take the longer route too," I said in the end, while giving me more time to consider which job I would have later.

"Taking the researcher this time, maybe I am able to start healing and not concentrating on the symptoms," he said. I wondered if he would have ever chosen that in the real world if there had been an option to make it for his own kind of pharmaceutical industry, which just didn't follow the usual order.

"Well, it's my turn now, isn't it?" I looked at the map and tracked the three alternatives I could choose from above: lawyer, doctor, or engineer. Very well. I remember the last time Nathaniel hired a lawyer, but would I follow in Deen's footsteps as he did in previous years?

"I take the engineer," I said, and everybody looked at me like they were seeing a ghost.

"What's wrong with being an engineer?" I was a little obsessed by their expressions. It was a job where I could be creative while needing mathematics for the static and holding of a building. I liked it. It is almost as logical as a human body's functions. It might involve some decision-making too, but I couldn't find a single job there that you completely excluded. It was something I had to learn and get used to, but somehow I started not to take it as such a huge thing. Never had I understood how simple it was for Nathaniel, since every choice we made could possibly be the end of a human life. This was the single aspect of being a doctor that I detested the most.

"I didn't know you were interested in construction," Deen simply explained, and Nathaniel continued their "worries." "There is a lot of media included too." He teased me about all the drawing equipment and calculations, which made me roll my eyes and shrug.

"I hadn't imagined to be able to remain free from whose electro stuff my entire life either," but that wasn't entirely true because I worked hard to avoid having to interact with any of these people.

I could rely on logical facts derived from the environmental impact such devices had. The production and disposal of electronic devices contribute to environmental pollution and electronic waste.

However, this is primarily a matter of personal preference for me. I simply prefer analogue methods of communication and productivity, such as writing with pen and paper, reading physical books, or having a normal conversation instead of writing text messages furth and back. As a teenager, I have also learned about another point that I definitely wouldn't want to reach: the addictive nature of smartphones and laptops, particularly social media and gaming apps. That cannot be healthy in the long run. Additionally, I don't see the point in such external relations. Also, living without phones and laptops is a way to simplify life and reduce dependence on technology. There, I would rather cultivate deeper connections with others than be a bot.

In this game, nobody would give birth to any children. At the start, Nathaniel ran far away from us, but as soon as the game continued, we would catch him up. Together, we would make it to the goal. However, in the end, it was the amount of money that mattered to win. While he counted, Deen was already excited.

"842 000," he said proudly after he had finished counting. "It might be because I always offered you all the food and a free place to sleep," Nathaniel said, while we all started to laugh.

"540 000" I explained my sum, which wasn't enough to win but still too much to bring to a grave. In the end, everything would be of no use to me. I never had children. It could be donated to any kind of organization, not just the state.
"843 000," Nathaniel explained, and Deen's face fell from a proud smile into disbelief.

"That cannot be true. Let me count that." Nathaniel reached for the game money while he was smiling, amused by his reaction. After Deen had counted the money three times, he gave up and let him win the game of life again. Just this time, we are all more similar. Everyone managed their finances effectively until the game's conclusion, and they did so nearly simultaneously. Hopefully that would be the case someday in real life too, but that was nothing to have in mind or overthink since we couldn't change it anyway.

For the rest of the flight, everyone did a little bit of what they wanted. I read a book while Deen had fallen asleep, and Nathaniel went through the comments, reactions, and other news about the article that had been released.

"Look at that, Lusie," he whispered to me as he stood up and approached me with his computer. It was a video he wanted to show me, and as I saw who it was, my eyes widened in surprise.

"You are cancer-free now, I have heard," the reporter asked my patient, who nodded with the charming smile he mostly had on his lips.

"Very true. My father chose, luckily, to bring me to this clinic. I had bone tumours, and the public hospital informed me that while I might have a chance, I would never be able to resume my sports. At that point, my father acted for me and brought me to the natural healing clinic he had been reading about earlier. What can I say? After three months of their treatment, wonderful and kind doctors, I will be released by next week already and come back in the next season as planned." He was very good to talk in front of the public for his young age. The reporter smiled, supporting and nodding at each statement, telling him now how grateful he is that he will come back.

"Do you have any pain from the diagnosis still?" He asked, and instead of shaking his head, my patient tilted it to the left and right, reflecting on the pain he had endured and possibly still felt in some areas after the treatment.

"I am fine; there is nothing that is as painful as it was at some points earlier. The harshest thing for me was maybe the psyche at the beginning, but my kind doctor, Lusie Amans, would really stand by my side and guide me through that journey. It really was alike; people wouldn't just care about me because of the money they earned from their patients, but rather because they saw us as human beings, teenagers who had their own wishes and problems. It may not have even changed my point of view on the world, but it has also given me new motivation and the wish to support not only this but also other natural healing clinics in the future. Without their treatment, I probably wouldn't have lived anymore by now. With it, I am as new as I could be, more motivated than ever before to start to work out more both physically and mentally." His words, especially as he mentioned my name, made me shiver while a tear swelled up in my eyes. It was hard to find a more beautiful thing that had ever been done for me. Just such a "simple" gesture, at least for him, which just had to snap with the fingers before some reporters would hurry to catch an interview, but still, it was so much more. Not only did he pledge to assist us in the future and during this interview, but he also expressed his deep gratitude for our work. It warmed my heart and gave me not only hope, but also the ambition to look forward to treating every patient with my entire capacity.

"Is there anything you might want to say to the world before you continue that last week here?" the reporter asked while the patient nodded with a huge smile on his lips, like he had been waiting for that question to come.

"At first, I want to thank everybody at the clinic over and over again. I will never forget what you have done to help me; it really meant the world to me. Additionally, nobody comes from nowhere. Nothing comes from nowhere. Please treat your bodies well; it will help you a lot in the future to avoid coming into my position or getting any other self-made sicknesses. Trust me, you will also have a happier life."

Nathaniel tensed beside me as he spoke out the words *"Nobody comes from nowhere,"* and I looked sceptically at him for a moment. He assured me that there was nothing, but nothing wouldn't cause such a reaction. In the end, I was just very pleased with what he had been doing for me. The video showed that the phone started to vibrate like a bee, which flew around the world. It touched my heart and my trust in humans to start to think about what the pharmacists have been doing to them.

Chapter 15

The first day was over before we even landed. It was exactly 00:01 at this point, and we were all really exhausted from the flight. The first thing we did was also get to the "hotel." At least that was what I had been expecting while I heard about travelling to China for two weeks, which included a wedding and honeymoon. Apparently, that was nothing like what Nathaniel had in mind.

Nestled within the lush landscapes of the Chinese countryside, this luxury estate stands as a testament to elegance and opulence. Greeted by wrought iron gates adorned with intricate Chinese motifs, the grand entrance sets the tone for the magnificence that lies beyond. A sweeping driveway, lined with towering ancient trees and vibrant floral arrangements, leads to the main residence—a masterpiece of architectural splendour.

The facade of the mansion boasts a harmonious blend of traditional Chinese design elements and modern sophistication. Roofs adorned with intricately curved eaves, carved wooden panels, and ornate lattice windows pay homage to ancient Chinese architecture, while sleek lines and expansive glass walls add a contemporary touch. The exterior is clad in rich, earthy tones, complemented by accents of gold and jade, creating a captivating visual spectacle that exudes refinement and prestige.

Stepping through the grand double doors, we were greeted by a majestic foyer adorned with a shimmering crystal chandelier that casts a warm glow over the polished marble floors below. The foyer opens into a palatial living room, where soaring ceilings and floor-to-ceiling windows frame panoramic views of the surrounding landscape.

Every detail of the interior design reflects the utmost attention to craftsmanship and luxury. Intricately carved wooden furnishings, hand-painted silk tapestries, and antique Chinese artefacts adorn the living spaces, creating an atmosphere of timeless elegance and cultural richness. Plush velvet sofas, adorned with silk cushions embroidered with delicate patterns, invite guests to relax in comfort and style.

The gourmet kitchen is a chef's dream, equipped with state-of-the-art appliances, marble countertops, and custom-designed cabinetry crafted from rare, exotic woods. A formal dining room, with a table set for twelve, provides the perfect setting for lavish dinner parties and intimate gatherings alike.

The master suite is a sanctuary of serenity and indulgence, featuring a king-sized canopy bed draped in sumptuous silk linens, a private sitting area with panoramic views, and an en-suite marble bathroom complete with a Jacuzzi tub and a steam shower.

Beyond the main residence, the estate boasts an array of luxurious amenities, including a private spa and wellness centre, a fully equipped gym, a home theatre, and a sprawling outdoor terrace dotted with lush gardens, tranquil water features, and al fresco dining areas. It offers the perfect retreat for relaxation and entertainment amidst the beauty of nature. I was illuminated. How much did he spend on two weeks of holidays? It seemed like what I would have needed once in a lifetime.

In every corner of this luxury estate, from its meticulously landscaped gardens to its exquisitely appointed interiors, the fusion of traditional Chinese aesthetics and contemporary luxury creates an unparalleled oasis of sophistication and refinement. It left me breathless, yet I was a little impressed and flattered.

"Accepted?" Nathaniel wrapped his arms around me while I stood there, watching the noble luxury exterior terrasse.

"You have to be kidding!" he chuckled for a moment behind me, while I almost felt like I couldn't breathe anymore. We had previously been in many luxury hotels, but, convinced by this place, they were shabby.

"We will do exactly this for almost two weeks; let's go to bed for now," he said, gently taking my hips and leading me to the bedroom, where Deen had already been falling asleep. At first, he would also express his astonishment over how Nathaniel could rent such a place, but it wasn't convincible to me. I said nothing at all at the start because I thought that he was kidding. That was too much to be true. Yes, we wouldn't have much time for travel in the future, at least not longer than about two weeks, but still. This was more for a king and queen than three doctors, who are going to marry tomorrow.

It was already tomorrow. The time had passed too fast. Despite the passage of the entire day, I felt as though I could neither breathe nor eat because I knew I would soon be required to fit into Barbie clothing.

Even if it was a lot of excitement to come to this place, it wouldn't take longer than a few minutes for me to fall asleep in Nathaniels securing arms.

The next morning, we stood up at the same time. We had been sleeping very long, including Deen, who had already had a head start from the flight. It was almost twelve a.m. when we woke up. It had been years since I had been sleeping for such a long time. However, we were served breakfast with everything you could imagine. The breakfast was still typical Chinese, featuring a variety of herbs and fruits. I could imagine why Nathaniel was so fond of this country, too. Their lifestyle was more like ours than the typical one at home.

The rest of the day, we were there together all the time, and aside from that, a young Chinese woman guided me to my clothing room for tomorrow. Yes, I did get my own room for that day. I already saw my dress in there. I was never interested in clothes; I almost hated shopping and would just take whatever I got in the end. As I saw this dress, I dwelled at once upon the idea that there was nothing illuminating about dresses.

Imagine a wedding dress that embodies purity, elegance, and luxury in every detail—a gown that captivates with its simplicity yet enchants with its refined sophistication. This exquisite creation, crafted from the finest silk and delicate lace, is a vision of timeless beauty and understated glamour.

The woman who had guided me here suddenly started to talk about the dress too. "You see that it begins with a sleek silhouette, gently hugging the curves of the bride's body before cascading into a voluminous skirt that pools gracefully at her feet. The bodice, adorned with intricate floral lace appliqués, creates a stunning focal point, drawing the eye to the bride's radiant smile and luminous complexion.

The neckline is a study in classic elegance, featuring a subtle sweetheart shape that accentuates the bride's décolletage while remaining modest and refined. Delicate cap sleeves, adorned with hand-sewn pearls and Swarovski crystals, add a touch of sparkle and whimsy, framing the bride's shoulders with ethereal grace. Despite its regal appearance, this wedding dress is designed with the utmost comfort in mind. The lightweight fabrics and expert tailoring ensure ease of movement, allowing the bride to dance and twirl with effortless grace throughout her special day. The gown's impeccable craftsmanship and attention to detail provide a sense of security and confidence, allowing the bride to focus on the joy and celebration of her wedding day. "Do you like it?" was the simple question that caught me off guard in the final moments. I had never envisioned myself as the kind of woman who meticulously planned her wedding from the beginning of our relationship, treating it as a significant historical event. Well, I was not—it had been Nathaniel who planned everything, even that dress, while he had been taking care of everything I had been saying before about whether I liked it or not. Others would just nod while it went in the left and out of the right ear. He captured the smallest details and tried to create anything I would be comfortable wearing tomorrow. The mere act of liking it paled in comparison to the emotions I experienced. Therefore, I just nodded while tears swelled up in my eyes.

"You are insane." As I ran in his direction, I nearly collided with him due to my inability to halt in front of him before landing in his warm embrace. He laughed amusingly, gently guiding me back into a standing position.

"It is my pleasure that you look good. It is me who chose it; you will just fit into it better than that one there," he pointed with the head at Deen, who was trying to touch the fish in the small lake in front of the house. It was a truly unique experience, and in such an opulent setting, you had the freedom to do anything you wanted.

I gave him a soft kiss, but I had to stand on my toes to reach him. His smile conveyed an expression of protection, power, and dominance, as well as joy, and for that, I appreciated what he had planned. Maybe there is also a little pride in that.

It was already diner time again. To have my own cook was something I would never decline. It gave us more time for ourselves, whereas we were just there to be informed once the meal was finished.

"As a starter, we have "Buddha's Delight," which is a vegetarian dish featuring a medley of seasonal vegetables, including bamboo shoots, mushrooms, water chestnuts, and lotus roots, stir-fried in a fragrant sauce of soy sauce, ginger, garlic, and sesame oil." They bring delicate porcelain bowls to each of us. While explaining what it was. Luckily, it was not that much, since it was just the start of tonight's dinner. Still, it was one of the best meals I ever had. They shared this opinion with me.

"The next one is Braised Abalone with Sea Cucumber; considered a delicacy in Chinese cuisine, abalone and sea cucumber are braised together in a rich, savoury sauce made from oyster sauce, soy sauce, Shaoxing wine, and aromatic spices," the woman explained while handing it out to each of us again. If that were the case for the next two weeks, maybe I could not enter the private jet. Even if everything was healthy, I wasn't a person who could eat a horse every day. I ate very slowly, and maybe not as much as others.

"As a desert, I chose Longevity Peach Buns for you today, which symbolise longevity and good fortune." These delightful, steamed buns are in the shape of peaches and are stuffed with sweet lotus seed paste or red bean paste." Although we received the food once more, my hunger had been satisfied. Still, it was like a shame to refuse what surely had cost a fortune. On the other side, he had demanded that he decide everything himself. That concluded for me: I should stop overthinking and convincing prizes with the amount of money I had in my past life and finally let it go completely. In the end, I was a girl who had come a long way through many boundaries to now live the life she wanted. Not deserved. Nobody deserved anything. We had come and would go in the end; whatever we did was our choice, and there was no guarantee that we would get anything out of it. We were free in every normal way, which meant that we should never expect anything in return. I learned that some years ago, my life got better at once, accepting but also limiting what I would do to please others. Without that, I rarely found any pleasure in it. Money was just a piece of paper—important, but nothing for me to keep in mind every single day. Happiness, on the other hand, had the power to keep me awake during the darkest nights without requiring any thought or spell.

"Wake up, darling." The next morning, I was kissed awake by them both. It was the most beautiful way to start the day. I was surrounded by the individuals I cherish, and in the near future, my spouses will also be present. We started to eat breakfast, but then we had to depart ourselves the last time before the ceremony started. This was the final occasion before I became a married woman.

"You look wonderful," my stylist said as she transformed me into a queen based on the rich, beautiful clothing. The dress fit like it was made for me. Maybe it was even true; I could imagine that he had been spending that much money on this too. Additionally, he had considered another fact: I did not like to sit for hours and be dressed or use make-up at all. We needed just one in total.

Afterwards, they guided me to the place where the event would happen. For the past few months, I've been looking forward to this every second. However, I began to feel a sense of uncertainty about my decision-making abilities. In the end, there was just the bureaucratic part, which changed for us. Still, it seemed like a straightforward task. On the other side, what was I dwelling upon?

Nathaniel had been helping me with everything, from starting a life I loved, healthy and without the bounds of my past, to showing me ways of feeling pleasure that I hadn't imagined existed, and finally giving me the opportunity to study and now work at the clinic. Deen had also shown me a lot while helping in his own way; at first, it was him who brought me to the clinic, and later, he helped me to say goodbye to the biggest part of my past too. He would lead me to find another hotter place to live, even if Nathaniel would be in charge for both of us most of the time. I learned a lot from them, and they helped me go step by step to the life I always wanted. On the other hand, it was my feelings that mattered, not what they could do for me with the money they had. Luckily, these were even clearer than everything they had done for me.

As I went to the altar with Nathaniel and Deen on each side, I was shivering. Endorphins flooded my body, and the only thing I wanted was to be even closer to them than they are right now. Nathaniel stood to my right, while Deen stood on the opposite side. Unlike his brother, Nathaniel simply scanned our goal, making sure I wouldn't fall into the shoes I was wearing. It wasn't that I was not able to go in, but it was the most uncomfortable part of the outfit, even if it was not high at all.

As we walked further, I realised that the ceremony was not what I had anticipated; it was not just for us but also included some guests. In the end, the twelve chairs may not have any meaning. Nine guests were there, sitting in two rows while they watched us. Coco and Abigail, whom I got to know at the pharmacist clinic, are now free. Gloria Devenson, Alice's mother, sat beside Coco, holding each other's hands, while they were already there sobbing.

Amandus Morgan, who had been Nathaniel's lawyer but was a former friend of Deen's family, Also, Richard Gardiner, the former leader of youth welfare, was a cancer patient when I first met him, but he helped Nathaniel for many years to come away from the streets. Additionally, three of our closest friends, each from the BDSM scene, sat in the public square and smiled towards us. My heart beats faster, showing me how alive I am. The suffering had vanished; just my ring from Jake remained from those hard times. The only person who wasn't present but might have been, given his location on this planet, was Alice. Otherwise, Alice, who also should have been here, was the last to die at the former clinic. Our close companion passed away several years ago.

As we stood in front of the priest, who was clad in flowing robes of azure silk and whose presence commands reverence and respect, I somehow felt better. With a voice as soft as a summer breeze yet imbued with the wisdom of ages, he began the ceremony with a solemn invocation, invoking the blessings of the heavens upon this union of souls.

"Beloved friends and honoured guests," he started, his words carrying the weight of centuries of tradition. "We gather here today to witness and celebrate the union of Lusie, Deen, and Nathaniel in a bond of love and devotion."

He pauses, allowing the gravity of the moment to settle upon the gathered assembly, before continuing, "In the sacred journey of life, we are blessed to find companions who illuminate our path, who share our joys and sorrows, and who walk beside us through every twist and turn of fate. Lusie, Deen, and Nathaniel have found such companions in each other—a union of hearts that transcends the boundaries of tradition and convention."

With a gentle smile, the priest turns to Lusie, Deen, and Nathaniel, his eyes alight with warmth and compassion. "Today, you stand before us not as individuals but as partners in a shared journey of love and discovery. May your hearts be filled with compassion, your minds with wisdom, and your souls with boundless joy as you embark on this sacred union together."

He extends his hands in blessing, invoking the divine forces of the universe to bestow their blessings upon the newlyweds. "May the blessings of heaven shower upon you like raindrops on a thirsty earth, nurturing and sustaining your love through all seasons of life." May your union be a beacon of light in a world shrouded in darkness, illuminating the path for all who seek love, acceptance, and understanding."

With a final benediction, the priest concludes the ceremony, his words echoing in the hearts of all who bear witness to this sacred union. "Lusie, Deen, and Nathaniel, may your love be as enduring as the mountains, as vast as the oceans, and as boundless as the sky. May you walk hand in hand, side by side, through the tapestry of life, weaving a story of love, laughter, and limitless possibility." A tear of pleasure slid down my cheeks as we did the same thing we had done at the proposal.

I kissed Deen, while Nathaniel hugged the two of us. Our bond grew, never to be broken. Wherever we came from or who we had been before, right now we are there. A trio will be united forever. As long as we existed, we dedicated our lives to the clinic and each other. Forever.

Preface

Thank you for continuing to be part of their story. It may have been deeply emotional and touching, or it may have even prompted you to reflect on our society today. That was exactly the purpose of the entire series.

If you want to hear more from Lusie, Deen, and Nathaniel, I would recommend you stay in touch and start to read the next book series', called "A First", which will lead you through the life of a named character in this book.

As the young cancer patient said, stay healthy and take care of yourself so that we can see you again many other times in our regular meetings in the book.

Have a wonderful day,

your L.H.K.

That was the "One last…" series

One last **B**eat

One last **D**eath

One last **S**uffer-ring

One last **M**istake